Katie.com

>>> *My Story* >>>

Katherine Tarbox

ORION

An Orion paperback

First published in Great Britain in 2000
by Orion Media
This paperback edition published in 2001
by Orion Books Ltd,
Orion House, 5 Upper St Martin's Lane,
London WC2H 9EA

First published in the USA by Dutton, a member of
Penguin Putnam Inc

The publishers wish to make it clear that the author of
Katie.com, and the events described in *Katie.com*, have
no connection whatsoever with the website found at
domain name and address www.katie.com or with
the email address katie@katie.com

A CIP catalogue record for this book is available
from the British Library.

ISBN 0 75284 298 6

Printed and bound in Great Britain by
Clays Ltd, St Ives plc

To my mother, Andrea Tarbox
For her wisdom, courage, strength, and love

CONTENTS

>>>

Katie.com

Me, Before

>>>

I can't tell you what all thirteen-year-old girls are like, but I can tell you what I was like. Of course, this was all before.

>>>

I was in the eighth grade, and for the first time I was really obsessed with my appearance, my status, with fitting in. This is understandable, if you consider that I was growing up in America, and in New Canaan, Connecticut. New Canaan is the richest town in the richest state in the country. The moms all drive Suburbans and the dads all take the train to the city. And by the time they are ten years old, the kids in New Canaan know that the highest-grade BMW is not as nice as the best Mercedes. They know that you should never be seen cutting your own lawn, and that embossed stationery is far superior to lithographed.

On the surface, everyone and everything in New Canaan is tasteful. We don't have any fast-food restaurants or neon signs because the town doesn't allow them. The houses are all the same—colonial, wood siding (never vinyl), two stories. In general people are friendly and pleasant, and it seems like the most serious thing that ever happens in New Canaan is the cancellation of a ladies' tennis match.

I have a love-hate relationship with the town of New Canaan. I love it because it is beautiful. The best of everything is available, from chocolate to people, but after everything that happened to me when I was thirteen I began to think a little differently about what the place had taught me about myself and about life.

>>>

The first thing you notice about the people in my town is that almost all of them are good-looking. In fact, being pretty is so common in New Canaan that the only people who stand out, the ones other people point at and talk about, are the average-looking ones.

Since I was very little, I have been confused about what beauty is and what it means. At thirteen I accepted the image of beauty I saw on the covers of fashion magazines. I thought the Calvin Klein models inside were beautiful. I thought ultra-thinness was beautiful. Beauty was painful. And it was very expensive.

I am sure that I started thinking this way when I was thirteen, because that was the first year I noticed that most of the really bright and successful people I met also happened to be beautiful. I wondered which came first, the beauty or the success. Perhaps their looks accelerated their success, or because they were successful they had the money to invest in their appearance. No matter what the cause, you can see that beauty equals success right on TV. And I don't just mean actors. Even the people who do the news on TV are attractive. Think of Diane Sawyer or Stone Phillips.

In New Canaan, there were plenty of beautiful rich people walking the streets as living examples of success. It seemed like all the women were blonde and slim with perfect skin and perfect hair. Their children were pretty, too, and a lot of effort went into making sure of this. I was always surprised when I met a kid with a less-than-perfect smile who didn't have braces. Everyone in New Canaan had to have impeccable teeth to go with their perfect hair and unblemished skin.

I managed to meet the size-ten weight limit, but I knew I fell short of most of New Canaan's beauty standards. In an effort to catch up, I read every single beauty magazine I could get my hands on, certain that inside lay the secrets to a successful, happy life. I would buy at least five magazines each month, usually *Marie Claire, Mademoiselle, Allure, Self,* and *Glamour.* After reading these I would then trade them to my friends in exchange for magazines I hadn't purchased. This way, I could read the whole magazine rack. Though a casual observer may think these magazines are alike, they are not. One might have one hundred suggestions on how to do your hair or how to pluck your eyebrows for proper shaping and contour. Another would offer reviews of the best tanning products. I felt like I needed every scrap of beauty information available, and I worried enough about missing something important that no magazine page was left unturned.

There was a problem with the magazines, however. Some of the articles gave conflicting information, which led to confusion. As *Glamour* encouraged me to wear makeup, *Mademoiselle* told me that most of it is made with whale blubber, a little fact that made me sick.

Then there was the problem of my own inner standards. Despite all of the influences around me, I also believed that for a person to be beautiful, she had to be *naturally* beautiful. The glow had to come from within, not out of a bottle. The trouble was, deep down, I knew I didn't possess natural beauty, and if makeup was cheating, then I was doomed to be ugly. And because of this, I was going to have limited choices in life. Now that I am a few years older, I know I am not ugly. But back there in the land of thirteen, I could see that I wasn't the airbrushed Calvin Klein ad. I wasn't even close. And since that was beauty, I was the opposite.

>>>

Being afraid that I was not beautiful didn't prevent me from putting a lot of time and energy into my looks. I wouldn't leave the house unless my hair was blown-dry to make it perfectly straight. This took time, and since I sang in a select chorus at school—rehearsals were at 6:45 A.M.—I had to get up before dawn to do my hair. The teacher's rule was if you're late, then screw you; the door will be locked and you'll surely hear about it later. I was never late.

Because I wasn't the most quiet person when I woke up, I usually made noise just walking the few feet from my room to the bathroom. I don't know how I did it. My mother claimed I slammed the doors, but I believe these were hyperbolic statements. (When I was thirteen, *hyperbolic* was one of my favorite words, and it seemed like everybody was a little hyperbolic.)

I thought spending large amounts of time in the bathroom was frivolous. I didn't take long in the shower, and I never spent time looking at my body because I didn't like it. I kept a towel around me until I entered the water, avoiding the mirror at all costs. If this meant standing under the shower with cold water on my head for a few seconds until it got warmer, then fine. I got in there, did what I had to do, and left. I did everything to conserve time. I brushed my teeth in the shower, a trick I saw in a movie once. And if I had to shave I did it very quickly, taking a razor and running it up and down my legs. I didn't use any of those prissy shaving gels. Altogether, I spent only about a minute and a half in the shower, but believe it or not it took me a long time to learn how to tie my hair up in a towel after showering. I am still not sure if I do it right, but the way I do it works. I love my hair; I wouldn't trade it for anything. It is blonde and straight, and I wouldn't want it any other way.

>>>

After I showered I inspected my face for blemishes. I learned in *Marie Claire* that the best time to pop zits is right after a shower. This is because the steam from the shower opens your pores so the pus drains easier. I couldn't stand to leave zits on my face. I never had a lot of them, though the occasional few did come along and needed proper attention. If I didn't take care of them, my mom was sure to say something, which was a lot more painful than any squeezing could ever be.

As I was finishing up in the mirror I'd turn on the radio and then the hair dryer. I'd think about my outfit and sing along.

I love music, almost all types. When I was little, we rode in the car singing songs by the Rolling Stones, the Beatles, Buddy Holly, the Temptations, and my mom's favorite, Rod Stewart. I know all the words.

I also like some new songs. I can beat anyone at name-that-tune, even if you include opera and classical. Unfortunately I don't carry a tune very well. My mom says she would rather listen to a dying duck. My voice is really that bad. The only reason I got into all-state and the select choir was because I play the piano for some of the songs, so I'm not completely useless.

I didn't dry my hair in front of the mirror because, like I

said, I hated mirrors. I didn't put on hair spray or any styling products because I didn't want to take the risk of damaging my hair. I always wore it down, parted in the middle, cut on an angle so I'd have small wisps that hung in my face. This gave me the opportunity to play with it during the day.

I know you may be bored hearing so much about my hair, but this is what matters when you are thirteen. Besides, my hair was the only part of my body that I liked. I trimmed it every seven weeks at a salon to ensure healthy ends. I tried hard to never have a bad hair day. If I didn't have time to blow-dry it straight, then I didn't wash it. Going out with wavy hair would have been too embarrassing.

Once I finished with my hair I got dressed. If you were ever an eighth-grade girl, then you'd understand how much I focused on what people wear every day. I have always liked clothes, but at thirteen I was absolutely obsessed with them. Without telling anyone, I tried to set a record for wearing a different outfit every single day. I really don't think I actually made it through the whole year, but I wanted to go as long as possible. At the start of the year I planned out my clothes so I could go at least four months, maybe four and a half. I figured at that point my parents would take me shopping, and I was right.

I had two rules about making my outfits. One involved shoes. Even though they do make the outfit, an outfit wasn't a "different" outfit just because I wore different shoes.

Number two: I wouldn't resort to wearing anyone else's clothes, or wearing something that was very old. Even if I had never worn it. I had a teddy bear vest that I had never worn. Even so, it was old, so it was against my rules to use it to make a new outfit.

I guess you could say my style was perfect for a middle-schooler living in Martha Stewart country. It was all J. Crew and Gap. Khakis, oxford shirts, polo shirts, sweaters tied around the neck. Solid colors only, no prints. Nothing else really passed—except for pleated skirts and argyle kneesocks. Most of my friends shared the same taste. We didn't wear hose. But we did wear jeans. I usually wore Gap special-edition jeans. My mother didn't understand that they were worth the extra ten dollars, but they were, because they came a little more washed and faded.

Everyone I knew was just as obsessed. Two of my classmates—Sandra and Erin—planned their outfits weeks in advance. They even created an exchange system for rotating their entire wardrobes.

Eighth grade was also the first year girls started to wear skirts and dresses to school. The girl next to me in social studies class always wore skirts when she was trying to get the attention of some guy. It was pathetic. I usually wore them only on gym days. That way I could slip my gym shorts on underneath and nobody had to see me in my underwear.

Which reminds me, I hated my legs then, just as much as I do now. At thirteen I already had the biggest thighs in the world. They were so huge that my mom wouldn't even buy me a skirt that was above the knee.

>>>

My whole morning routine took until 6:25. This was when I went into my mother's room and kissed her good-bye. It was usually the only time in the day when I saw her. Ever since my father left our family—I was a baby at the time—my mother has worked full-time. But when I was around eleven or twelve she really became a workaholic. Most of the time she got home so late I didn't even see her before I went to bed. She really lived at work, or for her work. Even if she was home, she was always thinking about work.

After I kissed my mom I went downstairs to look for my stepfather, David, who drove me to school. By the time I was thirteen, David and my mother rarely ever slept in the same bed anymore. David snored too much, so he slept in the guest room. David and my mother never took vacations alone as a couple, ever. And they argued like there was no tomorrow. Despite all of this, in some strange way that I can't figure out, they loved each other.

Like my mother, David was pretty much a workaholic. But even though he had a long commute to the city, he drove me to school early every morning so I could make chorus practice.

I didn't much like talking to David, so these car rides consisted of me changing the radio as much as possible. I couldn't stand to listen to bad songs, so station surfing was very big with me. Occasionally David said, "Can't you just leave it alone, Katie?" It was just a five-minute ride to school but I didn't stop pressing the buttons until I found something I liked.

>>>

Like most schools, I guess, mine was often frustrating and I felt misunderstood a lot of the time. The most alienating part of school is the way they separate you into groups, as if to say, "This girl will be a success, but this one won't." Like most kids, I never got into the program for gifted students, and it bothered me. We all knew what it meant.

Fortunately, there was one teacher I felt close to—the choral director, Ms. Montarro. She loved students who co-operated with early-morning call, and I did. Our group was called the Choraleers. Twenty-five kids from the seventh and eighth grades met three or four mornings a week. We mostly sang cheesy stuff, but we were pretty good. We sang the

National Anthem at Mets games, and we sang at the all-state convention and for Congress.

In school, I was probably most devoted to music. Outside school, it was swimming. In fact, by the eighth grade swimming had become the major focus of my life, and as a result the New Canaan swim team—a highly competitive, nationally known club—was a big part of our family's life. My mother was very friendly with the coach and the other parents. And my younger sister, Carrie, had started swimming, too.

I first got involved with swimming when I was a preschooler and went for lessons at the YMCA. Their system started kids out as "guppies" who wore water wings and splashed around the pool with their mothers. (I went with my nanny.) Swimming was an important safety thing in our family and my mother insisted we work through minnow, fish, flying fish, to the shark level, which was the highest, so we would all be able to handle ourselves in the water.

By the third grade I had noticed the swim team, which also worked out at the Y, and started to think that I might like to try it. Unlike other sports, which require a lot of hand-eye coordination—more than I possess—swimming is a matter of practice and commitment, two things I could manage. When I told my parents that I was interested in joining the team, they were excited that I wanted to participate in any kind of sport.

I began competing in the fourth grade, which meant I also started practicing many hours a week. The main feeling I had at those early practices was coldness. Swimmers move fastest through cold water, so the pool at the Y was always chilly. I was usually one of the last ones in, and I never got used to the cold.

The team competed mainly in regional meets, but every year we qualified for some national tournaments as well. I suppose it was exciting to travel to different meets, but the most I ever saw of any of the cities we visited would be the hotel, the pool, the airport, and, if I was lucky, a restaurant. It didn't really matter if I was in California or Florida, it all seemed the same to me.

I invested a lot of time and effort in swimming, so much that it became a big part of my identity. My parents got hooked into the swim team, too. At the pool there were always two competitions. The first was the actual swim meet. Even though we all wore swim caps and bathing suits, everyone knew each other, or at least the competition. I know I would sit there and inspect the muscles of each swimmer, how defined they were and well trained they looked. You couldn't hide any of it in a swim suit, and I had a pretty good idea about who was a serious competitor even before we got into the water.

While the swimmers competed on the pool deck and in the water, upstairs in the bleachers the parents were competing, too. They kept track of who was swimming when and what times were needed to be able to finish where. The parents were always talking with each other, trying to figure out who had done what. They wanted to know how much extra help a particular swimmer might be getting. Who had private lessons? Who had a fitness coach?

I always felt like my self-worth was determined by how well I placed. And I think the parents felt the same way—their status among the team parents depended on how well their child placed.

As I improved, I became one of the swimmers that the coaches depended on for winning times. Where once it was enough to be in the top ten, gradually I was pressured to be in the top five, four, three. All the emphasis on winning made swimming less and less enjoyable. During those moments when I had doubts about staying with the team, all the work put into swimming convinced me to continue. I shoved my doubts away and thought, If I don't swim, what will I do? I'll have no life.

>>>

When you consider the demands of swimming, choir, and school, it's obvious I didn't have a whole lot of time for friends. In fact, I had just one close friend, a girl named Karen. As far as I could tell, Karen had a perfect life. She was tall and thin. She had dirty blonde hair and blue eyes. She was a soccer player, and her team had won a regional championship. She was also very intelligent.

Karen lived in a two-million-dollar house. It wasn't as gorgeous as the house next to it, which was on the front of *Unique Homes*, but I would have traded it for our house in a second. It had so many bedrooms that her older sister was allowed to have two. The whole place was decorated like a shrine to a happy family. The walls were covered with pictures of vacations, soccer games, and holidays. I always wanted my mom to put up pictures of our family, but she said she didn't have time.

Karen's family was sort of like the Kennedys, without the politics. They were all smart, all excellent athletes. Her brother Rob attended Williams College. Her father was in the real estate development field, and her mother was a full-time homemaker. Every time I went to Karen's house, her mother was cooking something like chicken or pasta. And she would do anything for us, even run out and get a last-minute video. And I will never forget the hot fudge she made for special occasions like Karen's birthday.

It's funny; I didn't like Karen in elementary school. She was a tomboy back then. She even admitted to me that she wore boxers in fifth grade. But by middle school she was in most of my classes and it didn't take long for me to see that she was no longer a tomboy. In fact, Karen had a way with guys, and all I could think was that she had somehow learned it during her tomboy phase.

>>>

I couldn't approach guys the way Karen did. I didn't have her confidence. I knew I was not beautiful the way she was, but I also couldn't see what she saw in guys our age. The cliché about girls being more mature than boys is true. Just listen to boys talk. It's always about skateboarding or something they saw on TV. Girls talk about relationships and the future. Serious things.

I also didn't understand the idea of *dating* at our age. I mean, I thought a date was where a guy picks a girl up at her house and takes her out. How can that happen in middle school? No one has a driver's license or the money for going out to eat or to a movie.

Nevertheless, girls my age put a great deal of effort into somehow connecting with boys in a romantic and sexual way. I almost fell out of my chair in social studies class one day when I heard that a girl named Jenny had given a blow job to a boy named Adam at a local park. At first I refused to believe it. But I heard it from a reliable source, and Jenny was one of the short-skirt girls in our class. A month later she was reportedly actually having sex with another boy. I heard her talking about how she had used an orange-colored condom and how it felt to lose her virginity. I was so grossed out.

It wasn't just Jenny who was running the bases sexually. Rumors flew around school about who fingered who, and what guy managed to get his hand up which girl's shirt.

At parties we would play a game called *Never Have I Ever*. We would sit around in a circle with some type of alcohol or beverage. Someone would then say, "Never have I ever kissed someone," and everyone who had kissed someone would have to take a sip. This game made everyone's experience level in the sex department—or at least what they confessed to—common knowledge.

My experience was nil, and I couldn't decide whether this was embarrassing or not. One spring afternoon I was sitting outside on a concrete bench waiting for a ride home from school. It was late, so there was only one other girl waiting with me. I had never talked to her before, but I knew who she was. She always wore black tops—long sleeve, short sleeve, halter—always black.

It wasn't long before she asked me if I had a boyfriend. I wasn't even wearing a bra yet, and this girl wanted to know if I had a boyfriend.

"Are you kidding me?" I laughed. "We are much, much too young to be dating."

"What's the matter with you?" she said sarcastically. "We're not too young. Everybody's doing it. That's the way it is."

And with that, she turned away. I felt stupid because there was obviously something going on that I didn't know about. Luckily my ride arrived and I didn't have to sit there with her any longer.

When you are thirteen, you spend most of your time trying to figure out whether you're a kid or a teenager or an adult, when you are really part of each. You feel like people are constantly judging you for the most superficial reasons. No one my age seemed to be interested in music, or books, or any of the things that mattered to me. They cared more about who had big boobs and who was still a virgin. I was beginning to feel completely alone.

My Family

>>>

Before I tell you about my real family, let me tell you about my idea of what the best family is supposed to be like. I'll tell you right now that I know people who are like this, so don't say I'm making it up.

They are all-American-type people from San Antonio, Texas. They enjoy hiking and camping and family road trips. I wouldn't call them religious fanatics, but they do have a strong belief in God. They even keep their family photo album in a fireproof safe.

They are a lot of other things, too. They are good to the point of being disgusting. They don't swear. They never say they hate anyone.

I have never been to their house, but I imagine that above the fireplace they have a family portrait done at Sears with one of those awful blue backgrounds. In the picture the girls are probably wearing coordinated outfits—not the same outfit, but coordinated. There are two boys to balance out the girls in the family. Everyone is intelligent and works extremely hard, so they get good grades. They are all athletes, including the parents.

The family has a lot of home-cooked meals: barbecues, Sunday dinners, Tuesday-night tacos. They go on trips with other families. The parents don't have great jobs, but they earn a respectable amount of money. I guess they are middle class. I think the ideal family would be that, because too many times in my experience the rich get away with things too easily. In a lot of ways it is better, more wholesome, to be middle class.

Even though I had my own ideas about this "ideal" family, I didn't want any part of it. All I really wanted was for my biological parents to be in love and still married.

On many levels, my family is probably closer to the American reality than my ideal. Our relationships are complicated, and everyone is extremely busy. We are nothing like the people in the Sears portrait.

I am the middle of three sisters. Abby is four years older than me. Carrie is four years younger. Her father is David, my stepfather. Abby and I are both from my mother's first marriage, to a man who left her before I could even crawl.

Because my mother had to work hard to support us, for all of my life we have had various housekeepers and nannies. They did everything for us—cooked, cleaned, and ran all of our errands. But despite all their efforts I always wished I'd had a nanny like the one in the Harriet the Spy books. A nanny who would talk to me. Except for one, they never really seemed to understand me, plus they were always leaving and being replaced, so I never felt attached to or comfortable with them.

In addition to the nannies, we've always had a cleaning lady. My parents don't like cleaning (although they will do it when forced), and I have never been assigned chores because my parents don't believe in them. My mother's philosophy is that kids should be kids when they are kids—they have the rest of their lives to clean house.

>>>

When I was thirteen, I was much closer to Abby than I was to Carrie. Abby and I teased each other a lot. I made fun of her hair, which is curly and uncontrollable, like a perm gone bad. She made fun of my chest—which was size A—and, well, Abby was more than fully developed by the time she was fifteen. Abby and I also competed over height, but it didn't matter, because we were both short.

Even though Abby is four years older than me, everyone always thinks that she is younger. She has an innocent face—freckles, curly blonde hair, blue eyes, tiny nose—that makes her look thirteen even though she's now in college. Despite her appearance, she's able to handle herself in most adult situations, and I learn a lot from her. When I was eleven, we were allowed to go into New York City alone to see the musical *Damn Yankees*. Just being with Abby made me feel grown-up.

When we got into the city I was hungry. Abby was probably hungry, too, but we had exactly three dollars between us, so she was not about to buy me food. But I persisted with my complaining, and she eventually relented. We went into Starbucks, bought a small lemon cake, and split it. Afterward I was dying of thirst, but we were out of money. I ended up taking one of their printed advertisements and making a little paper cup so that I could drink the milk that was set out for the coffee. This might sound small, but it was the kind of adventure I had only with Abby. With her, I could be myself and have fun.

Over the years Abby and I have done most of the same

things, so it has been easy for my mother and my stepfather to compare us. Of course, we did it ourselves, too. I remember when I received my scores for the Connecticut State Mastery Tests. My mom suggested that I get out Abby's old scores and we laid them both on the table side by side. Mom insisted on comparing both the overall scores and those for the individual sections. She did it out of curiosity, not to pit us against each other, but I still felt bad as I realized I had the lower scores.

Even though Abby and I had fun times together in the past, our relationship has been at its best in the years since she moved out of the house to go to a private school in New Hampshire. With her gone, there was less competing, fighting, and arguing. Unfortunately, there was also less time for us to really talk. I wish Abby and I had had those talks about guys that you see sisters have in movies, but even back then I knew more about dating than Abby. Abby was seventeen and she had never been kissed. It wasn't because she was ugly, but because she was shy and didn't really care about dating. She was a very by-the-book type of girl, and that book would be called *How to Be a Good Girl*.

Abby's move to boarding school, which happened when she was fifteen and I was eleven, meant that Carrie and I were the only ones left at home. Suddenly the sense of competition shifted. Now Carrie and I were always comparing ourselves. I may have been the better student—that was clear—but Carrie had begun swimming at meets at a younger age than I had. When it came to swimming, she had the edge, and it bothered me.

My mother kept the score sheets that showed how we had done at each meet. Sometimes, if she really got going at it, she would make spreadsheets of our scores. No one ever came right out and said that Carrie was a better swimmer than me, but you could see it in the numbers.

Swimming was not the only area where the littlest sister had a real advantage. Carrie is the only one of us who is David's biological daughter, and this means she is the only one who lives with both of her real parents. To me it seemed like David favored her. I wasn't just jealous of his attention. It was more the fact that she had her actual father to talk to. To make things worse, like all my friends who had two parents at home, Carrie didn't seem to appreciate what she had.

When we were together, Carrie and I were likely to get into some kind of argument and it often escalated into pushing, shoving, pinching, or slapping. I think my jealousy contributed to our fighting, but it was never the specific cause. Usually it started when she did something that annoyed me—like crossing the invisible boundary in the backseat of the car—or took something of mine. This happened all the time with clothes. We raided each other's closets almost every day, and then argued over who took what and how it was or wasn't returned.

One of these times I came home from school to see her wearing my favorite white sleeveless oxford shirt from The Gap. She had never asked to borrow it and lamely explained that I had taken something from her room and therefore she was entitled to wear my shirt. This was probably true, but I wasn't in the mood to accept it. Arguing became yelling, and finally Carrie pulled out a blue permanent marker and scribbled all over the shirt while she was still wearing it. "You can have it now," she sneered.

You might wonder where my parents were when this kind of thing occurred. Usually they were out, but even if they were home, they often just told us to work things out ourselves. In this constant war, they would intervene only if things got physical. In the case of the oxford shirt, all my mother said was that she would buy me a new one. It never happened. And Carrie was never punished.

Sometimes I am amazed that Carrie and I are still living and breathing, considering how much we fought when we were younger. Although my grandmother says it is healthy for kids to fight, I think we pushed it to the limit. The funny thing is, our fights were usually about nothing. I guess that is why my parents used to tell me, "You have to choose your battles wisely."

>>>

The most influential person in my life is my mother. Just from the way my mother looks, you can tell she is very proper and demanding. She is tall, about five foot ten, and she is pretty large. She has always fluctuated in weight, but no matter what, I have always thought she was pretty. I guess everyone's mother is pretty in their eyes, but I truly believe my mom is a beautiful person.

My mother liked to talk about being a great pioneer in a male-dominated workforce. She said she helped break the glass ceiling, and I admired her success in the business world. Since she was the primary breadwinner in the family, she controlled the house with an iron hand. It was funny, though—she liked to talk about how much she hated men, but she acted just like them.

Even though my mom could be strict, she was also a mentor and a best friend. I love it when people tell me that I look just like my mother. We do look a lot alike, but I also hope the similarities run a little deeper.

I have always known that my biological father was pretty much an asshole. However, when I was very young— seven or eight—I didn't want to admit this to myself or to my friends. He and my mother met in college, and I like to fanta-size that they courted like the couple in *Love Story*.

My parents were separated and practically divorced before I was even conceived. It happened one weekend when my father came to visit with my sister and then stayed on for an extended period. My mother claims that she went along with it—planned it even—because she wanted to have another child and didn't believe that she would ever remarry. I wish that I had been conceived out of love.

As far as I can remember, I was actually in my father's presence just once, when I was about five. He had just met a woman he liked at his office, and I believe he was using my sister and me to impress her. He told my mom this woman was a real find because she had had her tubes tied. So, on a Saturday he picked up Abby and me and took us to an amusement park. For some reason he started calling me Kitty. He continued to call me that throughout the afternoon. At the end he bought each of us a stuffed bear. I got a white polar bear. I still have it. I'm not entirely sure why I've held on to it, because I know I felt as if I had spent that entire day with a complete stranger.

>>>

My mother married David when I was four. I didn't understand what marriage was then. And when David's par-ents came up to Abby and me and declared that they were our new grandparents, I told them we already had grand-parents and didn't need more.

I have always held a certain image of an ideal father in my head. It's based on what I heard about my friend's fathers. They took their daughters to baseball games, gave them clothes they wouldn't ordinarily get when they went shop-ping, and served them sugar for breakfast. David didn't do any of this, and whenever I asked him anything the reply was, "Go ask your mother." After a while I just stopped asking him. Going to David was a waste of time. This is why I have never considered David my father.

The thing that bothers me the most about David is that he likes to analyze my feelings over and over again. He says I am afraid of betrayal, so I never turn to him. I think that is a lot of bull. Why would I be afraid of being betrayed by him? Because my father left me? I was only a baby when my father left, so I have no painful memory of it. And besides, David had a clean slate. He could have defined what a father is for me. Instead he always told me to go to my mother for answers or for help, and she was usually working, so I was left on my own.

By the time I was thirteen I didn't think that I should have to respect all adults. I didn't disrespect them, but I was finding my own answers and a lot of what I was seeing and hearing about the adults around me was very hard to accept. I wanted adults to be perfect. I wanted them to be flawless role models, guides, even protectors. When you realize that most adults aren't perfect at any of these things, you begin to lose your faith.

Him

>>>

In the summer between seventh and eighth grades Karen began saying that we should have boyfriends. By the middle of the summer she had fallen "in love" with a guy named Peter. They had met on a weeklong bike trip with a youth group. I was happy for her, but I didn't see what she saw in him. He wasn't as bright as she was, and I thought people in relationships were supposed to be equals. And maybe it was just the awkwardness of thirteen-year-old relationships, but they never really seemed to talk about important issues and they didn't like to do the same things.

I was very confused. Karen and I had taken all of the *YM* magazine quizzes together to see if we had a crush on someone or if some guy could have a crush on us. Neither of us ever scored very high, but suddenly Karen was light-years ahead of me when it came to dealing with guys. She could talk about a movie in a way that captivated the most popular boy. She knew the exact moment to do the spontaneous flip of the hair, or the subtle glance, and when to brush against him as if it were an accident. Somehow she had learned the art of attraction while I was still trying to figure out what kind of boy I liked.

I thought I wanted someone who would share my interests—music, reading, movies—someone who was intelligent and kind and funny. Someone I could learn from. The problem was, middle-school boys had none of these qualities, and they were only interested in girls for their bodies. They examined girls under a microscope. They picked everything apart. Your hair, your eyes, your smile, your breasts, your waist, your butt, your legs. Everything could be either too big or too small, too jiggly or not jiggly enough. I once heard one boy tell another that he didn't like a girl because her nose was too big. I didn't think something like your nose should matter, and the fact that boys focused on such things was deplorable. But girls weren't much better. They saw guys as status symbols. It was all about image and whether you were attractive enough to get one that was handsome, or rich, or smart, or popular, or, best of all, all of the above.

Like I said before, New Canaan was a town filled with beautiful people and I was pretty much the opposite. So while Karen spent all of her time with Peter, I was trying to fill my time in other ways. That was when Abby came home for the summer and brought along her computer fully equipped with America Online. Suddenly there was an entire new world opening up to me in on-line chat rooms and the World Wide Web, and it was limitless.

I had seen America Online once before, at school, when our class did a science project on the Everglades. At that time, we had only used the Web for research. But I had heard all about the infamous "chat rooms" where you could talk to anyone around the world by sending messages back and forth. So I asked Abby if could use her computer, and of course she said yes. I had no idea what to expect, but I logged on and with a few clicks I was on-line.

It was unbelievable. The list of rooms covered every conceivable interest, and many I would have never imagined, including one called "sexual overdrive," whatever that meant. Many of the rooms were concerned with sex, but there were also teen chat rooms. These weren't divided into interest areas. Instead they were called simply TEEN1, TEEN2, etc. I thought that these would be the tamest areas and that I would stick to them.

When I first began chatting, my screen name was Atarbox, for Abby Tarbox. It was something my sister picked out. I hated having Tarbox in the screen name. Nobody else used their actual names. Their screen names were more playful or original like Phantom92 or Skywalker2. I planned to get rid of Atarbox as soon as possible.

Entering a chat room is like entering a party where you don't know anyone. You start by telling everyone the same thing over and over again: the basics about age, gender, location, interests. Inevitably things get around to sex and appearance. All the guys on-line say they are at least six feet tall with brown hair and blue eyes. They all describe themselves as if they are Tom Cruise's taller twin. And they all want to know what you look like, especially your body. You can be sure that every time you go on-line someone is going to ask you your breast size. I don't really see why anyone bothers to ask. Everyone lies when they answer.

It didn't take me long to figure out that a lot of the guys in the teen chat rooms were not normal guys. They were animals that just wanted to be excited by someone they thought looked like Cindy Crawford with a breast size of 36F.

Despite all of this—despite all of the weirdos and the

creepy feeling of being detached from reality—a small part of me believed that there was someone out there on the Web like me. I knew that this person wouldn't be easy to find, and he wasn't. Every time I met someone we'd exchange basic data and then search around for something real to discuss, but I would slowly realize we had very little at all in common.

As summer passed, what little bit of hope I once felt about locating a kindred soul in those chat rooms began to fade. But I didn't stop visiting. On most days I'd spend a couple of hours on-line. Usually my parents weren't home to even know what I was doing. When they did check on me, they warned me about giving out my real name and address or any information that would help a stranger find me. I wasn't worried about that. I would never take such a risk. Aside from these warnings, they didn't have much else to say. They trusted me, and they didn't really understand how big and broad the Internet was, anyway. Neither did I, but I was learning fast.

>>>

If I had a saving grace in my thirteenth summer it was the time I spent with Abby driving together to volunteer at a Boys and Girls Club that was about ten miles away, in one of the poorer parts of Stamford. Abby was one person who let me change the radio station as much as I liked. She sang along with me, and it was fun because she had a way of screwing up the words, too. Normally we talked about silly things, but that summer the church wanted me to decide whether I was going to be confirmed or not. Though my family hadn't taught me much about God or Christianity, I did know that I didn't want to be confirmed in something I didn't believe in.

So on those rides to Stamford and back, I asked Abby how she had decided that God existed. She couldn't explain it in a way that was convincing to me. She tried, but it always came down to a simple matter of faith. I needed actual proof, and in the end I decided that it would be hypocritical for me to go through with confirmation, since I really couldn't say I believed.

I wasn't disappointed that Abby couldn't convince me to believe in God. That wasn't what I was after. I just wanted someone I trusted to answer my questions. She did this for me. She took me seriously, treated me like an equal, and this made me feel closer to her than I had ever felt.

>>>

In the last week of August, Abby went back to school, and I started to face the fact that I was also going back to my own school routine. I wasn't going to have Abby to talk to every day. Instead, it would be just me, my parents, and my little sister again, living our mostly separate existences.

Moving to the eighth grade would be a big adjustment. Because of overcrowding I was going to have to go to New Canaan High School. I was going into a building where some of the kids were eighteen years old. They drove cars and had jobs. They were practically adults, while I was closer in age to elementary school kids.

The high school was a truly hideous concrete building, and to make things even worse, we were going to be crammed into classrooms in the basement, where the windows were few and the light was never sufficient. Although the walls were painted bright puke school colors, the floors were dark, which made the whole place feel cold. This is what I had to look forward to every morning when I got up alone to face the school day.

>>>

On the Sunday before school started, I was scheduled to spend the whole day swimming laps to raise money for our swim team. I woke up at 5:30 A.M., and I don't know if I was lonely or anxious about the new school, but I couldn't go back to sleep. Dressed in my pajamas, I walked into Abby's room and turned on the computer. (I had made sure to install AOL on it before Abby returned to school with her laptop.) I signed on and let it sit there for a couple minutes while I went down to get some cereal. I brought my bowl of Lucky Charms up and sat on my sister's bed.

Although I didn't know it at the time, I was actually one of the first users of America Online. I certainly was the first in my group of friends to use the Internet. It was 1995, and although most people had modems, I don't think many of them understood that some small internal computer thingy was able to connect them to millions of other computers. Most people, including my parents, were pretty ignorant about the Internet. The movie *The Net* had just come out that summer.

It's funny to think about connecting to cyberspace from Abby's room. Her walls were decorated in a Laura Ashley pink flower print, with a coordinating border. The curtains matched the walls, which matched the bedspread. It looked like a room at a bed-and-breakfast, except for the computer.

I sat there with my cereal, pointing and clicking my way to my usual destinations in the teen chat rooms. There weren't many people on-line that morning. I guess people weren't eager to talk so early on a Sunday morning. In fact, there were so few people that I was debating whether to sign off and go running instead. But I compromised and decided I would stay just a little bit longer, to see if anyone had any interest in talking.

Then I heard the small chime sound that signaled that I had an instant message at the upper-left-hand corner of my screen. Someone who called himself Vallleyguy—with three *l*'s—wanted to chat.

VALLLEYGUY: *Hi.*

ATARBOX: *Age/sex?* I asked.

VALLLEYGUY: *How old is the oldest person you will speak to on-line?*

ATARBOX: *27*

VALLLEYGUY: *That's good, because I'm only 23. What are your age/sex?*

ATARBOX: *13/f*

VALLLEYGUY: *Do you have any interests?*

ATARBOX: *I am a swimmer and I play the piano. I live in New Canaan, Connecticut.*

VALLLEYGUY: *I live in a valley outside of Los Angeles. I am pretty rich. I have sexy green eyes. Girls love to look into them. What do you look like?*

ATARBOX: *I have blue eyes, blonde hair, and I am short . . . What kind of music do you like?*

VALLLEYGUY: *Well, almost all types. And you?*

ATARBOX: *I love everything too. I have played the piano for 9 years so I like classical. I like new music too, but I hate jazz and blues.*

VALLLEYGUY: *Lol!* [laughing out loud] *Me too!!! But I especially like Mogart . . . Sry, Mozart. Do you like going to concerts? Do you go out on dates?*

ATARBOX: *Not really, I don't have time.*

VALLLEYGUY: *I love going to concerts. I just saw REM, and I love to go at least once a month.*

ATARBOX: *By the way, I am Katie.*

VALLLEYGUY: *Nice to meet you Katie, Mark here.*

ATARBOX: *Is it true what they say about everyone in LA being so into cars?*

VALLLEYGUY: *Yes. We live in them. I have three; a four seater Mercedes convertible--I love it--a BMW convertible, and a Jeep.*

ATARBOX: *I don't much care about cars. I think it is more of a guy thing.*

VALLLEYGUY: *How about clothes?*

ATARBOX: *I love clothes. I have a J. Crew obsession right now. But I also wear some Gap. I have some Ralph Lauren.*

VALLLEYGUY: *I wear Ralph Lauren, too. J. Crew is great as well. I just placed a large order there . . . but Katie, I have to go now.*

ATARBOX: *But why?*

VALLLEYGUY: *I am going to Miami to visit my mother. I like going there.*

ATARBOX: *Well maybe I will talk to you again some time.*

VALLLEYGUY: *I really liked talking to you. You're very smart. Maybe I can call you from Florida. Can I have your phone number?*

ATARBOX: *It's (203) 555-1234.*

VALLLEYGUY: *Okay, bye Katie!*

ATARBOX: *Bye.*

I really didn't expect that he was going to use my phone number. But part of me hoped he would. And I was excited that I had met someone just like me, but of the opposite sex. He even liked Mozart! At last I had connected with another kind, intelligent soul.

Best of all, he recognized me as someone different from

the typical thirteen-year-old. And though it may sound silly, I was impressed by the fact that he typed with proper punctuation and capitalized proper nouns and the first word of his sentences. Excellent grammar. A good vocabulary. I thought he *must* be all right.

Us

>>>

I swam hundreds and hundreds of laps at the swimathon. The lactic acid built up in my muscles and burned, and when it was over, I was so sore I could barely walk. My muscles got cold and stiff on the car ride home. When we got there, I literally crawled up the stairs to bed. I got under the quilt my grandmother had made—box squares in shades of purple—and immediately fell asleep.

When the phone in my room rang, it woke me out of a deep sleep. It also scared me. It was well after one A.M. Fortunately I had my own phone line, so no one else heard the ring.

I sat up and said, "Hello," with my eyes still closed. On the other end a very soothing male voice asked, "May I speak to Katie, please?"

"This is Katie." I lay back down on the bed.

"Katie, this is Mark from this morning."

"Mark. Why are you calling me now?" I thought he was crazy. It was so late. But I was also flattered.

"You said any time."

"I didn't mean that literally. I meant any time within reason. Why are you calling me?"

"Well, I have been thinking about you all day and I just thought why think about you when I can talk to you? So I figured I would call."

Now I was fully awake, and what he was saying felt good. It was exciting to know that he had been thinking about me, and I quickly forgot that I had been alarmed by his call. I bit my lip gently, and suddenly I didn't care what time it was.

"It is really hot here in Miami."

I told him I imagined that the humidity was terrible. "How was your flight?"

It was easy to drift into what I thought was a very adult-like conversation about travel. Mark said he had been to a lot of romantic, exotic places: Tahiti, the Caribbean, Hawaii. We talked about the Greek Isles. He hadn't been there, but he was eager to go.

Mark led the conversation, and I lay back in my bed and listened. I placed my hands on my white flannel sheets and buried my legs under the quilt. The room was lit by my Lava lamp, which I kept on at night. The glow covered my walls.

I was still sore, so I told Mark about the swimathon.

"I am an athlete myself, Katie," he said, explaining that he ran a 5K every morning. I was impressed. Actually getting out of bed every day, putting on the workout clothes, tying the running shoes, and taking those first strides requires genuine discipline. He said the Valley, where he lived, was pretty flat, so it wasn't a difficult run. He said that he didn't drink coffee, so a good run and a hot shower were his wake-up call.

No coffee. This was another thing we had in common. I like coffee ice cream, but I hate coffee. For a while in the beginning of the eighth grade I tried to force myself to like it. Having a cup of coffee. It seemed like a grown-up thing. I figured if I drank a little every day, it would grow on me. I tried dumping sugar—sometimes as many as ten packets—into it. Then came Carnation heavy cream and some half-and-half. I even tried half-coffee half-milk and I still didn't like it.

I told Mark all of this, and even told him about the cappuccino machine I had asked to get last Christmas. My mother got me all the cool attachments from Starbucks, so I actually had a pretty advanced setup with flavored syrups and a cinnamon grater. And my sister gave me a set of delicate espresso cups. Still, no matter how I tried, I couldn't make myself like it. The funny thing was, my parents don't like coffee either, so even they didn't drink my espresso creations.

Our little one A.M. talk was a lot like one of those getting-to-know-you chats on the Internet. We skipped quickly from topic to topic, trying to get to know each other. I loved the sound of his voice, deep and soft. Alone with him while the world was dark and sleeping, I felt like I was involved in an intimate little conspiracy.

It was hard to believe that this was the first phone conversation that I was having with Mark because it felt like I was talking with an old friend. But there was also something excitingly illicit in this moment. I wasn't oblivious to the fact that I had to go to school the next day. And I was aware that if my parents woke up and heard me talking, it would be a difficult situation to explain.

I always feel terribly guilty about breaking rules, and while I had never been told "Don't use the phone after midnight," I knew it was inappropriate. If my mother heard me, she would want an explanation. And I sure didn't want to explain why I was talking to some twenty-three-year-old guy from California I had never met face-to-face. I felt a tightness in my throat. It was just a little bit of guilt, flavored with the fear of getting caught.

Knowing that a mature woman would never say she was worried about her mother knocking on the door, I didn't tell Mark any of this. Instead I said I was tired, it was very late, and I had to go. I asked him to e-mail me when he got home and told him I was looking forward to when we would talk again. Feeling warm and happy, I hung up the phone thinking about all the things we had in common.

>>>

At 5:30 A.M. the clock radio alarm blasted me into a new school day with the sound of Mariah Carey's voice. Her album *Daydream* had been released that fall. I can't say I was fan, but it was all the radio played. Corduroy was the fad that September. In fact, it was all I bought from J. Crew. Corduroy pants in hunter green and blue. I also bought two jumpers that looked cute with white turtlenecks, white tights, and clogs. Although *Cosmo* gave specific details on whether or not you could pull off white tights, and theoretically I couldn't, I still wore them, even though I regretted it when I got to school.

All of this went through my mind as I dried my hair. I began to think about how I was an eighth grader preparing for another day—another year—of adolescent scrutiny, but just a few hours earlier I was talking to a man, a real man from California, who was truly interested in me and what I thought and felt. Thinking about Mark, I smiled, turned off the hair dryer, and picked up my mascara.

Eighth grade would be the year of makeup. Some girls caked on the foundation. Some girls brought huge Ziploc bags of it to school to apply in the bathroom in the morning after their parents dropped them off. Others came adorned with a little shiny lip gloss and mascara.

I used what I thought was fun to apply, but I tried to

keep it to a minimum. I was a Revlon fan. My friends and I decided we should have a signature lipstick color. We figured that if you see someone wearing the same lipstick all the time, you will gradually believe that it is the true color of her lips.

There was so much to be concerned about—hair, eyes, lips, nails. Eighth grade was the first year Hard Candy nail polish came out, and it was very difficult to find. It was a major stroke of luck when I managed to find some at Nordstrom. Not only did I get the polish, but I got one of those plastic rings that came at the top of the bottle. I had one with a blue star. Once that blue star was on my finger I grabbed my book bag and I was ready to go.

At school I thought about Mark but didn't mention him to anyone. I knew in my heart that after our late-night conversation I would hear from him soon. But days would pass and I would hear nothing. I resisted the urge to contact him. I'm not sure why, but it was important to me that he be the assertive one.

>>>

By the first week of school, Karen's summer-trip guy had become a real boyfriend. But instead of just going off with him, Karen made us a group. Instead of our usual Friday nights—talking, magazine quizzes—we went to the movies, the three of us. I felt pretty out of place, but every week Karen assured me that I had no reason to feel this way.

I don't know if this sounds immature, but I also felt awkward with him riding in our car. Sometimes my parents drove as part of the car pool rotation, and I hadn't had guys ride in my car before. Plus my mother's favorite thing in the whole wide world was saying things to embarrass me. I rode to the movies and back afraid of what she might say.

During the week I followed a set routine. It started with getting up alone, going to school, and singing with the chorus. Then it was on to classes which, for the most part, were either boring or ridiculous. I took English, history, Latin, and geometry, and for an hour of the day we participated in an experimental program. One day we might do crafts, the next, improvisational theater, or we might learn CPR. We also had woodworking and home economics. I never really felt like I belonged to any school, and in the eighth grade this feeling grew stronger. I think a lot of kids felt this way because we weren't in the middle school anymore, but we were by no means part of the real high school. We were just eighth graders in the basement.

As grim as it was, my return to school was not the only difficult challenge I faced that week. A new challenge began when I saw the look on Karen's face as she entered the cafeteria that first week of school. I was seated on one of the little blue stools that were connected to the table. It was the type that could easily fold up as a whole table and sat sixteen. My legs were crossed, I was sipping Diet Coke, and we were all complaining about how lame our classes were. Karen carried the little cloth bag her mother always filled with leftovers from dinner the night before, everything from macaroni and cheese to quesadillas.

She leaned against the table but couldn't quite look me in the eye. "Katie, come to the bathroom with me." I got up and followed her across the gray-speckled tile floor of the cafeteria, asking her what was the matter. "I'll tell you in the bathroom" was all she would say.

Though she was acting weird, I didn't think I was facing anything all that serious. I thought that maybe Peter had dumped her. But that was nothing to stress over, as far as I was concerned.

We entered the bathroom, and I was surprised when Karen said she actually had to pee. I waited, looking at the discolored white sinks. The paper towel dispensers had rust at their corners. The sinks and faucets were so cruddy, I could never be sure if washing my hands was a good idea or not. I mean, just turning on the water was bound to expose you to a community of germs the size of the state's population.

Karen walked out and turned on the water. She looked up as if she was telling me something ordinary and then said, "Rob has leukemia."

Leukemia didn't really register in my head as a deadly disease. And Karen's brother, who was about to enter his senior year at Williams, was so young that I just couldn't imagine him getting something really terrible. I fumbled for something to say.

"Is he going to be okay?" I finally asked.

"He is going to be fine, Katie. He is going for chemo this Friday. There is no possible chance that he is going to die." Karen wiped her hands with a brown paper towel.

The truth was, Rob wouldn't be fine. Karen's mother had already called my mother to tell her that Rob's condition was quite grave. He had a serious form of adult leukemia for which the survival rate was not good at all. But I was led to believe that death wasn't a possibility, because they caught the cancer in a routine physical very early and he was getting treatment. Karen was fed the same deception. Her parents didn't want this to affect her education, soccer, and the rest of her life. Later on it would be obvious that it was a mistake to lie to us. It's hard to understand why the same parents who always tell you to be honest lie about the most important things. It never works.

Even though I didn't really understand leukemia or Rob's case, I felt there was something serious going on. I wasn't going to pretend that it was simple like the flu. That night I made it a point to talk to Karen about it. I wanted to be a good friend; however, Karen was insistent upon not talking about Rob. She had already gone over it and over it too many times. She was also tired of having to say everything would be okay, because then it made her question her belief that this was the truth. I told her I would do anything to help her. The best thing I could do, she said, was to wait for her to ask to talk.

>>>

That fall our swim team began extensive underwater training. Practices were like military camp, or perhaps an extended version of pledging for a sorority. We did everything they asked us to do.

One of the major goals in swimming is to keep the number of breaths you take to a minimum. Breathing slows you down. To train our bodies to need as little air as possible, we did a lot of underwater work. We would sprint freestyle for ten laps, until we were good and exhausted, and then do a flip turn followed by two fifty-yard underwater laps without a breath. If you came up to breathe, they made you do another underwater lap. I would struggle under the water, feeling like I was about to pass out, but refuse to surface. I always made it, but others got into trouble. Once the coaches had to pull a girl out of the water who was so blue they had to revive her.

We all tried as hard as we could to comply with the coaches' demands. We did everything they told us to do or else suffered verbal humiliation. Or worse. Worse happened to me on a fairly regular basis when one particular coach—Judy—came up from Florida to put us in line.

Judy was a demanding, screaming kind of coach. She

would sit by the side of the pool with a canister of racquet balls in her hand, waiting to throw them at us. If I was too slow, or took too many breaths, or swam the wrong combination of strokes, she would bean me with one of those balls. Right in the head. At the same time she would yell something like "You idiot! Do the combination!"

You might think it was strange for the YMCA to allow this, or for a bunch of young girls to accept it, but it happened to almost everyone and after a while it just seemed normal. The chair incident was not normal, though. It happened late on a Friday night. Everyone was tired. I had had a lot of balls hit me that day. Judy was on the side of the pool near me, and she was getting more and more upset with something I was doing wrong. Out of the corner of my eye I could see her pick up a metal folding chair and come toward me.

"Katie Tarbox!" she screamed. "Get your act together now!"

She then threw the chair into the lane closest to me. I stopped, sort of shocked, and just looked at her. Everyone looked at her.

"Go get the chair off the bottom of the pool," she said. And that was it. Another girl helped me get the chair up from where it lay, eleven feet down, and no one said anything else. Even my parents. When I told them about it they laughed a little and said it was good the chair didn't hit me. I think they believed I had done something to deserve what had happened. I know that they thought that Judy, who had been on the national team, was there to help us. She knew what she was doing, and it was all supposed to make us winners.

It was typical New Canaan. Train. Compete. Succeed. And make it look easy. Though I didn't realize it at the time, we received every bit of extra help that was available because our parents and coaches could afford to give it to us. The head coach of my team, Mrs. P., was extremely wealthy. Her husband was vice chairman of a huge company and had stock that did incredibly well. She didn't really coach, but without her—and her husband's money—we would have been nothing. Mrs. P. paid to bring nationally known coaches and swimmers like Judy, many with Olympic experience, to New Canaan, where they would spend a week or so training us. She also arranged for us to go to Olympic training facilities in Colorado and Lake Placid.

Kids on other teams had to earn money to pay for these kinds of extras. They had fund-raisers—spaghetti dinners, bake sales, car washes. The Santa Clara team in California had a big bingo hall where the mothers worked. It all sounded like fun to me, but we never had to do any of it. Either big corporations gave us the money, or our parents just paid for things. My parents even arranged for a personal trainer to come to our house a few times every week to help me train with weights.

His name was Doug. He'd come to our house two or three times a week and we'd work with weights in the basement. I did a lot of repetitions, at low weight, for endurance. Doug told me what I should eat—a lot of carbohydrates, but not refined sugar—and he would measure my body fat, which was always too high. When we weren't focused on the work we did together, we talked about everything under the sun. Doug was attractive, so much so that he probably drove some of his women clients to distraction. But what I liked about him was that he spoke to me as if I were an equal. I found it easy to feel like we were friends. When I was twelve, and I was still considered to be someone with a big future in swimming, I thought it was cool to work out with Doug. But by eighth grade, as it became clear to me that younger swimmers were passing me by, I was thinking it was a bit too much.

As far as the adults were concerned, nothing was too good for New Canaan's swim team. Mrs. P. hired the same speaker that the New York Giants football team used for inspirational talks. He was over six feet tall, had brown hair, and was an ex–baseball player. "You have to have goals. You have to envision yourself reaching those goals. You must have weeklong goals, monthlong goals, year-long goals to reach your aim." I didn't go home and write down my goals, as he recommended. But I did think about what he said.

Unfortunately, no amount of inspiration was going to change the fact that at the age of thirteen I was beginning to plateau as a swimmer. When practices resumed in September I began to notice that the coaches were losing interest in me. I was getting less private time with them, and they were shifting their attention to other, younger girls. They were always interested in the girls who had the most potential. They develop a master plan, which they did for me, with the goal of making you a national champion. If it looks like it might not work out, they drop you.

Knowing all this, and suspecting that they were in the process of dropping me, I began to hate swimming more than ever. Of course, it wasn't as simple as that. I mean, I had made such a commitment to the sport, and to the team, that I constantly questioned my own feelings. I got down on myself for feeling bad about swimming. I even worried that there was something wrong with my attitude. After all, we were winners and all the coaches were having fun. Maybe my feelings were wrong.

Wrong or not, my hatred of the pool grew stronger as fall wore on. I began having nightmares about it. My biggest fear was that someone would see me naked, so of course I dreamed about being seen naked in the pool. I didn't quite know how I got there without a suit on, but there I was standing in front of everyone naked. I didn't know what parts of me I should try to cover up with my hands. Should I grab my chest or cover the southern part? Even in my dream, I was most upset about the idea that the other girls would be talking about what happened, how I looked, how I acted. I awoke full of anxiety.

Fear of being completely naked seems like a pretty universal thing, but some girls I know are so adjusted to the locker room that they will strip down without a care. They would just drop their clothes to the floor and walk to the shower. These girls weren't necessarily the ones with perfect bodies. They just didn't care.

Not me. When I undressed, I managed to keep a towel around me at all times, carefully shifting it so it fell down to cover any strategic area that was about to be exposed. When it came time to get dressed, I just reversed the process, pulling clothes up under the towel so that they covered me before the towel had to be dropped.

This fear of nakedness was just one of the anxieties and frustrations that I kept secret as I began training for the local meets that would help us get to national meets in the spring. There were both senior and junior nationals, U.S. open, and age-group nationals. We went to all of them. At each meet, the team's performance determined seeding for the next one.

Practices seemed endless, and since I always got yelled at, the pool was a very loud place. The screams from the coaches pierced through all the other sounds of the pool—the waves slapping the sides, the hum of the filter system, the echoes of voices. Most of the time I couldn't figure out why I was being chastised. And I kept thinking that since I was pretty good at this—I had actually won some pretty big races—it didn't make sense that the coaches would work so hard to make me miserable. Maybe I was just an easy one to pick on. Or maybe it was because I did talk back on occasion. That fall, when I was alone, I began to cry about swimming.

I was frustrated with the hours, and it ruined my social life. I didn't have time to attend the Friday-night parties that Karen talked about. I especially longed to go to the girl ones, where I knew all the juicy conversations were happening. I was always invited, but could never go. My parents didn't hold me back, but swimming did.

I was missing key opportunities to compare myself with people my age, to talk about what was ahead of us in high school, and to try to figure out if I was normal. After all, I had very few sources for this kind of information. Karen was heavy into her "relationship" and her brother's illness, and I was too busy to spend much time with other friends. Abby was gone from home, and serious discussions with my parents about this kind of thing were not really on the agenda. As a result, like a lot of kids, I found that TV offered the only steady stream of data. I knew it wasn't all reliable. But it was there.

I watched *Beverly Hills 90210* or *Melrose Place*. I would laugh at the episodes, but at the same time, I thought that the characters were showing me what life was really like in high school. The kids were mostly either jocks or babes. And there was one girl—Andrea—who was really smart, but not beautiful like the others. No one ever asked her out. You get the message.

Of course, none of the high school girls I knew had a full body like Brenda's on *90210*. But I thought that the situations and relationships on the show were probably close to the real thing. I was looking for signs of the future. And I thought that the show would apply to my life because it was set in Beverly Hills and we lived in New Canaan, which was a lot like Beverly Hills.

Before my mother worked so much, we used to watch these shows together on her bed. I loved those times. She always said that she watched in order to censor what I saw, but I know she liked these shows just as much as I did. She never censored anything. It was kind of funny, though. Right before someone hopped into bed, she would say something like, "That is so bad." I would then tell her it wasn't appropriate for her to watch and *I* would cover *her* eyes.

By the time I was thirteen, there was hardly ever any time for us to watch TV together. That fall Carrie and I would watch TV and eat dinner. David came home around eight o'clock, or later. Sometimes he would yell hi as he walked up the stairs, and my mother arrived home long after. September, October, and November were her worst months at work, because of a dreadful thing called "year-end." Because she worked on the financial side of the company, she was responsible for composing a year-end report. Sometimes she would come home as late as one in the morning, and she went to the office on weekends.

The combination of work, school, and extracurricular activities meant family time came second. Home was a place where I always felt alone.

>>>

I thought about Mark a lot. I dwelled on our conversations, his intelligence and his maturity. It was rare, at thirteen, to know someone who knew how to carry on a real conversation. And more and more, I thought our meeting on-line was destiny.

It was about a week and a half after that first telephone call, the one that took place in the dark before morning, when I swallowed my pride and sent Mark an e-mail asking if he had left the face of the planet. I got nothing back.

Days passed with no word from him. I began to lose interest, and when it got to the point where I just didn't care if there was a reply, I finally got one. It was a little note that explained that after Miami he had gone to New Orleans. He told me a story about partying on Bourbon Street. I was disappointed to hear this, so I told him I would write in the next few days.

ATARBOX: *You may think I'm a prude for saying this, but I think drinking and smoking are disgusting,* I wrote to him.

VALLLEYGUY: *Katie, everything's fine in moderation.*

ATARBOX: *All I know is that there were alcoholics in my family and they've done a lot of damage.*

VALLLEYGUY: *I'm not like that, Katie, believe me.*
When I asked what else he had done in Louisiana, Mark's response surprised me.

VALLLEYGUY: *I spent time with a girl I know down there. She's really great. Fourteen. She's a little like you-- smart, mature for her age. She's very sophisticated.*

ATARBOX: *Uh-huh* was about all I could write back.

VALLLEYGUY: *Of course she's not as sweet as you are Katie. I have never enjoyed talking to anyone as much as I enjoy talking to you. It's something rare. Something special, this kind of connection. Don't you think so?*

ATARBOX: *Yes, I do.*

VALLLEYGUY: *I want to ask you something, Katie.*

ATARBOX: *Okay.*

VALLLEYGUY: *Are you a virgin?*

ATARBOX: *I'm thirteen, what do you expect?*
VALLLEYGUY: *I really wish there was some way I could get to Connecticut to see you.*

After we signed off, I thought about the things in the conversation that seemed peculiar. The fourteen-year-old girl in New Orleans. Him flying there to see her. And why was he so interested in coming to Connecticut to see me? We barely knew each other. Was he serious or just being sweet?

I never said anything to Mark about these issues. Confronting him would have been awkward, unsophisticated. And I wasn't sure I had the right to question him about anything. He never asked me about anything sensitive, either. It was as if we both decided that anything that was too upsetting, anything that broke the positive mood, could simply be boxed up and put away like wool sweaters in the springtime.

>>>

After that conversation we began sending e-mails to each other on a regular basis, at least once a day. They weren't lengthy. The main idea was to keep in contact, maintain the relationship. I was very curious about him and his past. But as much as he asked me about my life, he said almost nothing about his own. Nothing about his friends or what he did on weekends. He said he liked sushi and to go to concerts. On a few occasions he discussed movies but never revealed who went with him. He also seemed to take many vacations, but he never told me who accompanied him. I didn't feel I was at liberty to ask, either, because I didn't want to come across as nosy. In the back of my mind, however, I wondered how he spent his free time. The only conclusion that I could arrive at was the possibility that he was a workaholic. I imagined he was brilliant, sensitive, and lonely.

At the moment, we were only friends, but it seemed to me that we were moving toward a deeper relationship, and that one day there might even be an "us" to talk about. Yes, thirteen was much younger than twenty-three. But in ten years that kind of age difference wouldn't mean anything at all. In my mind I went back and forth on this issue, trying to reconcile our age difference with what we shared in our hearts.

ATARBOX: *Don't you think that our age difference is a little weird?* I asked one October night.

VALLLEYGUY: *No, no, Katie. In other countries no one would even care. Americans' views are distorted when it comes to older and younger people and their involvement with each other. I mean, in France this would be perfectly acceptable.*

ATARBOX: *But we are not in France, Mark.*

VALLLEYGUY: *Well, I am not concerned about it, so you shouldn't be either.*

ATARBOX: *I guess you're right.*

VALLLEYGUY: *I know I'm right to care about you the way that I do. How could that possibly be wrong?*

As a child growing up, I had spent the great majority of my time in the company of adults. When a new nanny arrived, I was expected to take the initiative to show her around New Canaan and teach her the ways of the house. At school and at swimming, teachers and coaches dominated what was going on. Then I would work with my piano teacher and my personal trainer. Time with kids my age had to be arranged in advance so that everyone's schedule could be accommodated. This didn't happen very often.

All my life I had been required to trust adults, even

complete strangers, and in the safe confines of New Canaan that trust had never been violated. Mark made it clear he wouldn't say another word on the matter of our age difference. He had no problem. I figured that if I was truly mature, I would be unfazed, too. I never brought it up again.

Any lingering, unspoken doubts I felt about our age difference vanished whenever I talked to him. When we were together, Mark wasn't twenty-something. I wasn't a thirteen-year-old. We were equals who didn't really have ages.

Happy Holidays

>>>

Christmas is my favorite day of the year because we go all out for the holiday. Every year our family goes out to a farm on the day after Thanksgiving to cut down two large trees, one for the family room, the other for the living room. I always expect it will be very cold, so I put on long underwear, leggings, and jeans. I also wear about five shirts and three jackets. We all pile into the car and ride for an hour to the farm.

On the way, my grandmother usually talks about some weird bugs she has read about, or about her desire to make a car seat that can double as a toilet so that she can ride and not have to stop for the bathroom. Once we get there, picking out the trees is a free-for-all. I run around pointing to any tree that seems halfway decent, jump up and down, and scream, "I've found it!" I'm playing a game with myself and everyone else. Since I point to almost every tree, we always take home two that I discovered.

For a proper New Canaan holiday, the Christmas decorations must be "tasteful." We put a fresh garland around our light posts with small white lights. Our wreaths would never have bows in any colors other than red, green, and gold. My mother also has this weird obsession with nutcrackers. Not the little cheesy ones, but the noble-looking ones.

Once I asked if I could have one of those little Christmas village displays, but my mom said it was tacky. And another time I wanted to put colored lights on the tree, but you wouldn't do that in New Canaan, either, she said. When we were little, tinsel was allowed, but eventually it was banished, too. Now we put a select number of hand-painted or blown-glass ornaments on the family tree. Little white lights are discreetly placed within the branches of the tree, so the wires can't be seen.

Hidden in the family room, our second tree holds the more homey ornaments that Abby, Carrie, and I made over the years—construction paper wreaths with red scribbles, red Santas with cotton balls, stars made out of Popsicle sticks.

At Christmastime, family comes first, so usually we have lots of company, including David's parents and my mom's parents. My uncle Bob always comes. But on my thirteenth Christmas, for the first time ever, no one came to visit. My parents and sisters were a little depressed by this, but on Christmas Eve I went to sleep with the same feeling of anticipation I always had on that night. I awoke a little after three o'clock and knew I wouldn't be able to go back to sleep.

Since the crowd at our house was smaller than usual, I pulled open the French sliding doors to our living room expecting to be a little disappointed by the pile of presents under the tree. I was shocked to see how many packages were waiting there. I sat down on the hardwood floor. It was cold, but the excitement of Christmas morning—the smell of the tree, the sparkling lights, even the quiet of the night—made me feel warm. The packages waited for us, spread out in a pool of red, gold, and green. I began picking them up, feeling them and shaking them to determine their contents. Books were obvious. Clothes were squishy. But other boxes refused to yield their secrets.

In our stockings the wrapping paper was a bit more fun. For many years we had this Smurf Christmas paper, but that ran out. So we shifted to Barbie paper that came from FAO Schwarz.

Package inspection doesn't take five hours, and I had at least five hours to kill before anyone in my family woke up. I decided to go to the study because I loved the leather chair that we had in that room. It was an executive's kind, perfect for leaning back when you are on the phone. I always felt like sitting in that chair made me an important person.

When I sat down I decided to turn on the computer. It made two loud beeps as it started up, and, as usual, Windows took forever to boot up. The clouds flashed against the background until it finally dissolved into a *Lion King* scene that Carrie had installed for us. It was a picture of Simba.

I moved the cursor and clicked on America Online, which also took a long time to boot up. I think I was using a 24.4 modem, which was the fastest at the time. Even so, it took two minutes to complete the dialing, connecting, talking to AOL, checking password. I waited impatiently to hear "Welcome. . . . You've got mail."

I hadn't visited the teen chat rooms much since meeting Mark, but I decided they would be my best bet so early in the morning. I was very surprised to find Mr. Vallleyguy himself there in one of the chat rooms.

ATARBOX: *Hey, it's Christmas morning,* I wrote to him.
VALLLEYGUY: *Here too. Merry Christmas.*
ATARBOX: *What are you doing on-line?*

VALLLEYGUY: *I could ask you the same question, you know.*

ATARBOX: *But it's like 4 AM there.*

VALLLEYGUY: *I just got back from midnight Mass. I went with some friends.*

ATARBOX: *So how come you're not with family?*

VALLLEYGUY: *I'm alone for now, but I'm taking some time off to go to Florida to my mother's soon.*

ATARBOX: *That's horrible, being alone on Christmas.*

VALLLEYGUY: *I can't take your pity, Katie. Believe me, I'm all right. I kind of like the quiet.*

ATARBOX: *Well, I'm a big holiday person and I like a lot of people around. I like every holiday and all the stuff that goes with it; trees at Christmas, egg-dyeing for Easter, picnics on the Fourth of July.*

VALLLEYGUY: *What's Christmas like at your house?*

ATARBOX: *Santa always brings a big family present, and I wouldn't be surprised if it's a new computer this year. There's been a lot of talk about that possibility.*

VALLLEYGUY: *What about you?*

ATARBOX: *Believe it or not, I still have a Christmas list. This year I asked for a camera, Roller blades, books, CDs and clothes.*

VALLLEYGUY: *A friend of mine gave me an electronic dartboard. It's actually pretty cool.*

ATARBOX: *Really?*

VALLLEYGUY: *I played darts a lot in college. I was pretty good. We even played strip darts. It's like strip poker. The loser has to take off something. It was a riot.*

ATARBOX: *That's not exactly a Christmasy-type topic, Mark.*

VALLLEYGUY: *True.*

ATARBOX: *You went to Mass? That doesn't sound like you.*

VALLLEYGUY: *Well, I'm not into the religion thing. But I was raised Catholic and midnight Mass still gets to me. It can be a very beautiful ceremony.*

ATARBOX: *My grandmother's an atheist.*

VALLLEYGUY: *I can understand that.*

ATARBOX: *What are you doing during the holidays?*

VALLLEYGUY: *I will work like a dog. Maybe catch a few movies.*

ATARBOX: *Yeah, I think I will go see a few myself.*

VALLLEYGUY: *I just saw 12 Monkeys, it was horrible.*

ATARBOX: *I didn't see it myself. I hate sci-fi films.*

VALLLEYGUY: *I don't love them, but occasionally I will see them. I like action films more.*

ATARBOX: *I think I will go see Heat, because I love Al Pacino. I hear that it's supposed to be good. I hope I have time. I have to swim all week. It really pisses me off.*

VALLLEYGUY: *You have to swim all day every day this week?*

ATARBOX: *Yeah, it is so frustrating. I hate it.*

VALLLEYGUY: *Why do you do it?*

ATARBOX: *I wish I knew that myself.*

VALLLEYGUY: *It's hard when you are so good at something, but it also causes you so much trouble. Are you thinking about stopping?*

ATARBOX: *Not yet. I'm going to hang on. Maybe it will get better. Maybe I'll get a better attitude.*

VALLLEYGUY: *If anyone can handle it, you can, Katie.*

ATARBOX: *I appreciate that. I don't think anyone else would even listen to me say anything at all negative about swimming. They'd have a fit!*

VALLLEYGUY: *I'm here for you, you know that.*

ATARBOX: *I'm going to have to go pretty soon, so I can do the Christmas stuff with my family.*

VALLLEYGUY: *That's okay.*

ATARBOX: *I'm sorry you can't have a better holiday.*

VALLLEYGUY: *Katie, this chat makes this a pretty special Christmas already, and the sun isn't even up yet.*

ATARBOX: *I'm glad. Gotta go.*

VALLLEYGUY: *Okay. Check you later. Merry Christmas!*

Despite the chill in the house, I felt warm as I signed off. Mark was so open to hearing my feelings about swimming. It was even more important that he didn't judge me, or act like he expected anything from me. He seemed to understand and I became more and more open to him. I said things that I would never have said to anyone else. I knew he was a good friend to me.

>>>

While everyone else was relaxing during the holiday break, the swim team was scheduled for a week of daylong training sessions. Two of my friends on the team—Maribeth and Jennifer—would have to travel an hour each way from their homes to attend. To save them the driving, it was agreed that they would stay the week at our house. And I looked forward to their arrival, thinking it would break up the swimming week.

Maribeth was a thin girl and she and Jennifer were freshmen in high school. To me, high school kids were about as mature as one could get.

My mom used to shiver when she saw some of the things Maribeth wore—tight cutoffs with a tight silver latex-looking midriff top, heavy makeup. She wore her hair in a very high ponytail on top of her head, which my mom called a whale spout.

As different as Maribeth was from me, I liked her. On our first night together, my mom ordered in pasta from Prezzo, one of my favorite restaurants in New Canaan. After dinner we watched TV for a little and then went up to my room for bed. Between a trundle bed, a cot, and my own bed, the three of us fit in my room. It was a little tight, but it was worth the sacrifice so that we could all be together.

After five minutes of bitching about swimming and how long the week would be, we started talking about sex. Lying there in the dark you couldn't make eye contact, which made it easier to be open.

At thirteen I wasn't concerned about intercourse. I knew that unless I was raped, I was not going to do that before I was married or at least engaged. But I could foresee getting into a situation just short of the act itself. I wanted to know when in a relationship you were expected to let a guy finger you. When did you have to give a blow job? Was it assumed that you should just allow a guy you were dating to put his hands up your shirt? From what I had heard at parties, and from my other friends, I knew that some girls were doing these things, but I hadn't had a good live source of information since Karen had started going out with Peter and no longer had time for me.

Maribeth was by far the most experienced of all my friends. She went to the kind of parties where people experimented in these things, and she had done them herself. What surprised me was that she hadn't planned on any of it. She admitted to being fingered, which I found disgusting, and I wanted to know how she could let it happen.

Maribeth laughed and said, "It just happens, Katie."

I didn't want to believe it. I mean, it doesn't just happen

that a guy opens up your pants and then slips his finger into you, does it?

But Maribeth had no deeper explanation, so I changed the subject. I wanted to know how long this went on, and what you were supposed to do while he was doing this.

Maribeth explained that you just let him touch you and let him do it as long as he wanted. You were supposed to just sit there. I was having a hard time envisioning this. Were you supposed to get an orgasm from being fingered? I wondered. (Despite all the magazine reading, I wasn't quite sure what an orgasm was, but I was still curious.) Maribeth said no, you weren't supposed to orgasm. That only happened during real sex.

Now I was really confused. I had read more than once in *Marie Claire* that this kind of touching was a pretty sensitive, intimate thing. Maribeth didn't make it seem like that at all.

Maribeth wouldn't tell me if she was a virgin or not, because I think she was embarrassed. Anyhow, it didn't seem like her virginity mattered to her. In fact, I don't think it meant anything to her. I couldn't figure it out. She almost made it seem like you were just supposed to please yourself and that it didn't really matter if the other person was being aroused. That contradicted everything else I had ever heard or read, but in this area, she was definitely more experienced than me.

Through all of this discussion, Jennifer barely spoke. She had never had a serious boyfriend, nor was she one to kiss and tell. But she seemed just as interested as I was in what Maribeth had to say.

As I lay there listening to all the intimate details about Maribeth's affairs with guys, I said absolutely nothing about my own relationship with Mark. We were talking about sex, not relationships, and Mark and I were not sexual. Our relationship was more than something adolescent and physical. It was a deep friendship. And so I didn't tell them about him, but secretly, it made me feel more confident, knowing that I was involved with someone who was definitely interested in *me*, not just my body parts.

For some reason, I had trouble sleeping after my late-night talks with Jennifer and Maribeth. I woke up very early and couldn't go back to sleep. I'd go on-line. If Mark was there, I'd spend a long time chatting with him, sometimes sharing what I had discussed with the other girls. If he wasn't on-line, I'd write long e-mails to him. He was always interested in what I was thinking, and what was happening in my life.

As time passed, Mark replaced Karen as my main confidant. It wasn't something I planned. But I just never seemed to have time to be with her. I had swim meets on Saturdays, and that obligated me to have a good night's sleep the evening before. So it never seemed practical to go out on the weekends. I began declining invitations more and more, leaving Karen to find other friends. I felt bad about this, but at the same time I had made a commitment to my swim team.

I failed to see what was happening in Karen's life. I didn't think that her brother could be dying, and Karen said nothing that would make me think he was. After all, I was thirteen, and the biggest worry I had was finding the right outfits. Terminal diseases were not part of the world I knew.

Karen began to find new friends and spend time with them. I couldn't hate her for this, or even hold it against her. I had left her no choice. Still, I clung to the belief that we were best friends. Neither one of us said anything about the change, the pulling away. She never said, "Why don't we spend more time together?" I never said, "Karen, why can't you just talk to me about why you are so upset?" Our friendship just kind of ran out.

>>>

That January I caught the winter "bug" just as soon as school resumed at the first of the year. I either catch the flu or pretend to catch it every single winter. Most of the time I have faked it. It is pretty easy to trick the school nurse. I'd say that I had a sore throat and an earache. Usually one of my ears looked a little red anyhow. And since I have always had large tonsils, the chances were that if the ears were fine, my throat would look like I had some kind of bug.

If I knew I didn't have the symptoms to move the school nurse, there was always my mother. All I had to do was walk into her room, whine a little, and I was excused. It usually went something like this: "Well, if you really don't think you can go to school, then I guess you shouldn't go. But if you think you can go, then you should go."

I would assure her that, yes, I was sick, and that was it. I didn't do this a lot. I usually missed just ten days of school each year. I thought that that was a reasonable number of absences. And I don't doubt that my mother sensed that sometimes I was perfectly fine.

Unfortunately, this winter was one of the few times I was actually sick. And this year's flu was not the simple fever-and-aches kind. It was the messy, vomit kind that held me to the confines of my room and the bathroom for a week.

The only good part about the flu is that you can eat anything you want and not gain weight. Someone else might have just stopped eating altogether, until it passed. But I saw the flu as an opportunity to eat whatever I wanted, and in any amount. This time I chose to eat a lot of sour cream and onion potato chips. I don't think that they aided my recovery.

I was so sick that I barely talked on the phone at all, and I did not go on-line, which meant I didn't speak to Mark for well over a week.

When I felt better and I checked my e-mail, he was there, asking me where I had gone. After I told him I had been ill, he told me that he didn't want me to lose communication with him ever again for that long. He said that if he had known I was sick he would have called every day to make sure I was okay. I thought this was lame, and I was upset with him for not understanding why checking e-mail wasn't my biggest concern while vomiting all day.

But Mark was only expressing concern. He cared about me. That's what our relationship was about. He was a positive influence in my life, and I enjoyed being the only one from my world who knew Mark. He listened to my feelings about the people and circumstances around me. And he always supported me with encouragement and advice.

It was around this time that Mark and I exchanged pictures. He sent me some of himself at Disney World. I wondered who had gone there with him. After all, Disney isn't a destination you might expect for a single man. I wasn't impressed with his looks, but he was obviously a young, clean-cut guy, which was all that I really cared about.

I hid the pictures in my room, in the top drawer of my armoire, because I knew what they would look like to someone else who couldn't understand the connection we had made. And something in how Mark had complained about my short disappearance had begun to worry me. I began to wonder if we were getting too close. I know I was thinking about him more and more. I had followed my heart into this relationship, and it told me that this was a mature, adult friendship.

>>>

My connection with Mark grew stronger around my birthday, January 26. I was going to be fourteen, not an especially big milestone, but I was as excited as I had been at Christmas. In part this was because I was leaving thirteen, an age everyone seems to associate with teenage silliness. The night before, I tossed and turned in bed. For some reason I thought I would get to sleep faster if I buried my face into my pillows but that didn't work. Neither did adjusting and then readjusting the blankets.

I woke up at about two in the morning, and for the life of me I could not sleep. It was pointless to lie there awake when I could be doing other things, like making cupcakes to bring to school. I walked downstairs, being careful not to wake anyone. This didn't require too much caution. My mother wasn't even going to be home for my birthday. She was in San Francisco on business. David snores so loudly that nothing can wake him up, and Carrie has even slept through our alarm going off.

I went into the kitchen and I opened the light cherry cabinet doors. I found a box of Duncan Heinz cake mix, the super-moist type with the red background on the box. I am not much of a cook or baker, so this was perfect. Add water. Bake. Get a fairly reasonable cake.

I liked making the cupcakes myself. I liked the feeling of losing myself in a project—measuring, mixing, baking, putting on the icing. I also liked the way the oven filled the kitchen with warmth and a sweet smell.

I inherited a taste for cake batters and cookie dough from my mother. But we're not the only ones who like it. Karen's family used to make cookie dough without the eggs so that they could eat it while their cookies baked. This time I ate just enough to make myself a little bit sick before I poured the remainder into the little floured cupcake tins.

As I turned the timer I decided I would go on-line to pass the minutes until the cupcakes were done. I walked down the ceramic-tiled hall to the study and turned on the new computer that had arrived at Christmas. I watched the waving clouds as Windows began to boot up. I typed in my screen name, which I had changed to katie26, and waited for the connection. While I did this, I reached for a box of Godiva chocolates my parents had given me in advance of my birthday. I don't care for most of the fruity ones, but I love the white chocolate starfish swirled with milk chocolate and filled with hazelnut. Biting off each leg, I watched the computer screen shift from page to page.

When I finally got on-line, I followed my normal routine, which meant starting by looking for Mark. I moved the mouse over the pad, feeling the little trackball slide. I clicked my way to a teen chat room and checked to see if Mr. Vallleyguy was there.

KATIE26: *Hi Mark, it's Katie!* I wrote, seeing his screen name.

VALLLEYGUY: *Hey Katie, Happy Thirteenth Birthday!*

KATIE26: *Thanks, but it's Fourteenth you know.*

VALLLEYGUY: *I'm so sorry, of course it's 14.*

KATIE26: *No big deal.*

VALLLEYGUY: *You gotta stop growing up, because pretty soon you'll be too old and you won't want to talk to me anymore.*

KATIE26: *Impossible.*

VALLLEYGUY: *Isn't it the middle of the night there?*

KATIE26: *I couldn't sleep. I came downstairs and decided*

to bake cupcakes to take into school this morning,
for my birthday.

VALLLEYGUY: *What kind of cupcakes?*

KATIE26: *Just a mix.*

VALLLEYGUY: *I wish I was there to have one.*

KATIE26: *I'd give you one.*

VALLLEYGUY: *What do you want for your birthday?*

KATIE26: *I don't know. Christmas was so big, and it feels
like it was only yesterday. I think I might get some
clothes. My mother knows I'm in love with this gray
wool cardigan with embroidered snowflakes and
eye hook clasps. I wouldn't be surprised if she gets
it for me.*

VALLLEYGUY: *Are you having a party?*

KATIE26: *Not this year.*

VALLLEYGUY: *When I was a kid I didn't have parties,
but I went to some and they were pretty cool, I
mean, to kids.*

KATIE26: *I got to have some pretty big parties when I was
little. Not really fancy like some of the New Canaan
kids got, but they were fun. I could invite anyone I
wanted. No limit. In fourth grade I had a sleep-
over for forty girls.*

VALLLEYGUY: *Forty girls, WOW!*

KATIE26: *The noise was unbelievable.*

VALLLEYGUY: *A lot of squealing?*

KATIE26: *I guess so.*

VALLLEYGUY: *What are you doing this year?*

KATIE26: *Well, my mother is in San Francisco for business, so our family isn't going to do anything until
she comes back. Then we'll probably go out for
some special dinner or something.*

VALLLEYGUY: *Not on the actual birthday?*

KATIE26: *Well, the way the whole scheduling thing works around here we're pretty flexible about celebrating things on the exact day. It doesn't feel exactly right to me. But with my mother, you pretty much have to accept things.*

VALLLEYGUY: *So you're not going to have anything big on your special day, the actual day?*

KATIE26: *No.*

VALLLEYGUY: *Nothing at all?*

KATIE26: *Well, the cupcakes in school.*

VALLLEYGUY: *That's ridiculous. You should have something really good on your birthday, and I know what it should be.*

KATIE26: *What?*

VALLLEYGUY: *Why don't you come out here for the day?*

KATIE26: *What?*

VALLLEYGUY: *Come out to see me.*

KATIE26: *Mark, you're in Los Angeles, not New York. I just can't pop out to see you.*

VALLLEYGUY: *Actually, if you wanted to, you could. People do it all the time.*

KATIE26: *Fourteen-year-olds?*

VALLLEYGUY: *Some kids out here, like movie stars' kids, fly all over the place alone and it's no problem. You just call up a car service, let them take you to the airport, and then get on a plane and go to California.*

KATIE26: *For the day?*

VALLLEYGUY: *You can be here by twelve o'clock our time. You spend the day, take the red-eye back, and you're home in 24 hrs.*

KATIE26: *It really works that way?*

VALLEYGUY: *I can even call the car service and the airline, give them my credit card numbers, and it would all be paid for.*

KATIE26: *I don't have time to get ready.*

VALLEYGUY: *Look outside, Katie. It's 3 AM in Connecticut. You've got plenty of time.*

KATIE26: *What about when I get to Los Angeles?*

VALLEYGUY: *I'll meet you right at the gate. If you are really nervous about the time we wouldn't even have to leave the airport.*

KATIE26: *I'd really like to see you, but . . .*

VALLEYGUY: *Don't you trust me?* he wrote quickly.

KATIE26: *Of course I do. But how would I explain this to my parents?*

VALLEYGUY: *Tell them you're sleeping over at somebody's house.*

KATIE26: *What about getting presents here?*

VALLEYGUY: *Believe me, Katie, if you come out here I'll give you whatever presents you want.*

KATIE26: *I'm really flattered, Mark, but you know it's impossible.*

VALLEYGUY: *It's a nice little dream though, isn't it?*

KATIE26: *Yes. And when I'm older I'll probably do it all the time.*

VALLEYGUY: *It is like going around the corner, really.*

KATIE26: *So what's going on in your life?* I asked him.

VALLEYGUY: *I'm going to a Super Bowl party over the weekend.*

KATIE26: *Football is my least favorite sport, except for the Super Bowl halftime show. Remember when Michael Jackson did that heal-the-world thing? I was in fifth grade. I sobbed through all of it.*

> *Nobody lets me forget it, either. Every year around Super Bowl time the people in my family sing that song and ask me if I need a tissue.*
>
> VALLLEYGUY: *You know, football's an easy sport, and I could teach you about it, that way you could like it more.*
>
> KATIE26: *Did you play in high school or something?*
>
> VALLLEYGUY: *No, but I did date a few cheerleaders.*
>
> KATIE26: *Cheerleading is another sore subject with me.*
>
> VALLLEYGUY: *Why?*
>
> KATIE26: *I am totally against it. The little outfits make the girls into sex objects. And besides, women should play sports themselves, not just bounce around in response to men.*
>
> VALLLEYGUY: *I think you're wrong about some of it. I mean, some cheerleading is very athletic. They have competitions and everything. Look at the Dallas Cowboys Cheerleaders.*
>
> KATIE26: *I'd rather not.*
>
> VALLLEYGUY: *Okay, I get it.*
>
> KATIE26: *The cupcakes are done. I gotta go.*
>
> VALLLEYGUY: *Okay, Katie, when will we talk again?*
>
> KATIE26: *I'm really busy, but I'll look for you every time I'm on-line.*
>
> VALLLEYGUY: *Me too.*
>
> KATIE26: *Bye then.*
>
> VALLLEYGUY: *Okay. Bye birthday girl. Have a great day! I'll be thinking of you.*
>
> KATIE26: *I'll be thinking of you too. Bye!*

Our calls became an everyday occurrence, along with the e-mails. Talking to Mark was easy, and every day I looked forward to it. I was more open with him than I had been with anyone else before. I usually revealed much more about myself than he did, but this didn't bother me. I thought this was normal. From the articles I had read in women's magazines about how to get men to open up, I thought girls always divulged more than guys. I liked it that he listened, and that he was very funny. He had an intelligent sense of humor, which I found attractive.

VALLLEYGUY: *What do you like on TV?* he asked me one night.

KATIE26: *I know it's silly, but I love The Simpsons.*

VALLLEYGUY: *That's not silly.*

KATIE26: *But it's a cartoon.*

VALLLEYGUY: *The writing is actually very sophisticated. A lot of what they are doing is a spoof on other TV shows or things in society. I mean, Krusty the Clown is a takeoff on all those clown shows that were on TV when your Mom was a kid.*

KATIE26: *That's so weird.*

VALLLEYGUY: *But it's a parody. It's saying, Look at the violence that kids laugh at. Look at how they are manipulated to accept it.*

KATIE26: *I know.*

VALLLEYGUY: *Even the way Mr. Burns treats Homer is a commentary on work. Every time Homer walks into Mr. Burns' office, Mr. Burns can't remember his name. Homer's worked for him for years, but he can't ever remember his name.*

KATIE26: *And I thought I was immature for liking that show.*

VALLLEYGUY: *A lot of adults love that show, Katie. A lot.*

Talking to Mark always made me feel good. This made keeping him a secret all the more painful. He was the best thing in my life, and hiding him didn't feel right at all. I needed to resolve my growing feelings about Mark, one way or another. I was either going to have to give in to my growing feelings of love and affection, or let go of him. Soon I would be going to Italy on a school trip. I decided to use this time away from him to settle matters in my mind, and in my heart, once and for all.

Apart

>>>

Karen and I had signed up for the school trip to Italy in August, before we found out her brother was ill, before it became clear that we were drifting apart. When the time came to go, I hoped the trip would give us a chance to get closer again.

I also intended to use the time alone to think about Mark. I was a little worried about how much time we were spending together on-line and on the phone. When I told him I was going away, he wanted me to call him from Italy. This was too much. There was no way I was going to call him. Instead, without phone contact, without e-mail, I would reconsider the relationship without his influence. Part of me hoped I would decide he was not good for me. But I also knew that my feelings for him were strong, perhaps stronger than any I had ever felt for anyone before.

We flew from New York to Rome and then immediately on to Milan. After that it was a weeklong bus trip: Venice, Siena, Florence, Sorrento, Capri, Pompeii, and finally Rome. We saw much of the country, and it surprised me how diverse each region was, even in such a small area of land. It was not, by any measure, a vacation. I wouldn't call getting up early in the morning, visiting museums all day, and riding on a bus a vacation.

My favorite part of the trip was Capri, where we bought sandwiches and then walked up to a beautiful escarpment overlooking the sea. It had belonged to a Roman emperor who made criminals and enemies jump off the side of the cliff into the ocean.

As weird as it sounds, another of my favorite things about Italy was being able to get little green bottles of lemon-flavored Pellegrino. I fell in love with the sour taste and the soft fizz.

As I said, I had hoped that Karen and I would spend more time with each other, but we only shared a room for a few nights. Before we fell asleep, we indulged in what I call a little "girl bitch-out" time, which means we would discuss all the other girls on the trip. We nitpicked their clothes, recalled the annoying things they said, and made fun of everything down to the way they walked. One dorky girl, we called her "horse girl," couldn't stop talking about riding. In New Canaan you're supposed to be over horses by the time you're thirteen or fourteen. So Karen made her the target of our gossiping, which in some weird way was supposed to help us bond again. It didn't work.

>>>

I had hoped to forget Mark, but instead found myself thinking about him even more. As I sat on the bus with ear-phones in, my mind wandered to him. I thought about the way he made me laugh, and how he challenged me to think differently about life. He was the first person in my life who recognized that I had too much pressure on me. He made me look at how fast I had grown up and encouraged me to relax and have more fun. Whenever it snowed he would tell me, "Go out and build a snowman. Be a kid."

When he said these things, I felt as if he really cared about me, really saw what my life was like, what I had gone through. Maybe I had been doing too much. Maybe he could see me more clearly than anyone ever had. Thinking about this made me feel closer to him. It also moved me toward a decision about how I felt about him. At the start of the trip to Italy I was considering ending our friendship. By the finish, I had begun to think that what I felt for him was not friendship, but love.

The idea that I could love Mark and be loved by him was reinforced by my experience with Italian men. At home I knew I was not the prettiest girl and I worried about whether I was attractive at all. In Italy, the men made me feel that I was. I had heard that Italian men like blondes, but I had no idea what kind of attention I would receive. In Rome, Karen and I sat on the Spanish Steps sipping sodas and one man after another came up to talk to us. And they made me feel, for the first time, that I might be attractive in the way women are attractive to men, and that Mark might feel that way once he met me.

The confidence I got from this experience, combined with thinking about Mark nonstop for eight days, helped me realize that I loved him. I slowly decided I didn't really care that I felt no physical attraction. My feelings were deeper than that. I loved the way I felt when I talked to him. I admired his intelligence and sense of humor. I thought about his success as a person. And instead of feeling strong and independent, I felt that being without him was a struggle.

>>>

We flew home from Italy on the last Sunday in February. It was hard because it wasn't a night flight but instead one of those long day ones. I hadn't packed any books, so I had to pass the time with the onboard movie and music selections. The movie was *The American President*, which had some vulgar language in it. They edited out the F-word, which was hilarious because you could tell when Annette Bening was saying it, even though you heard something else. Karen and I found this ridiculously funny.

My parents were the only ones who met our group at the airport. Though the school had arranged for a bus to take us to New Canaan, my mother had decided to pick me up because Carrie was flying into LaGuardia around the same time and it was convenient to get us both. I was thrilled that they were coming to the airport. I was also thrilled to be going home to AOL, and to Mark

>>>

I didn't think that Mark would miss me while I was away, but I had hoped that he had thought about me like I thought about him. When I got home, I found an e-mail letter from him:

VALLLEYGUY: *Hi Katie!*
Welcome back! I REALLY missed you! Did you have fun?? I hope so. I'm anxious to hear ALL about IT! I'm kinda hoping that you called me. If not, that's still okay. I know you were busy.
The reason I don't know is that I'm in Miami, FL, not LA. I left the day after you left (Saturday), I left with my mom, and I'm still here. In fact, I'm writing you two days before you even get back. It's

*to let you know that I'm thinking about you, and
have been.*

    *I'll be in Miami the next couple of days, then,
before I go back, I want to fly up to visit you, ok? Is
that cool with you? Let me know.*

    *As soon as you get this message, let me know
when I can call you by e-mailing me. Let me know
exactly what time to call, and I'll call you to make
plans. I hope you're fine! Can't wait to see you!*

    Love,

    Me.

I smiled at the computer as I read it. It was the first time
I really felt love, or at least what I thought was love, from a
man. I wanted to see him more than anything in the world,
but I didn't think it would be easy to explain him to my
family. I sent back a lengthy e-mail, telling him that it just
wasn't a good time to visit. He replied with this:

VALLLEYGUY: . . . *I loved your letter, and would make lots
of comments now, but I REALLY want to hear your
voice and talk to you in person! I'm really having
strong feelings for you, Katherine. I finally know
that now. I know it BIG TIME!*

    *I can't get you out of my mind. You just pop
up in whatever I think about. And you know what?
It feels good! It really makes me happy inside just to
know that I'm thinking about you, and that the
most wonderful girl has entered my life.*

Knowing that he felt the way I did made our relationship even more comforting. We had both reached the same

conclusion when I was in Italy. We needed each other. I wanted to see him, if only there was a way.

>>>

Now that I knew how much Mark cared for me, I decided to tell just one person. It wasn't my sister or Karen. It was another friend named Ashley. I had grown closer to her as my friendship with Karen had waned.

I had known Ashley for a long time. We went to school together and swam together. Like me, Ashley had taken some time maturing. I guess that is what I loved about her. We didn't have long serious discussions about heavy topics. Instead, we spent hours jumping on her trampoline. Just like me, Ashley was the kind of girl that New Canaan never really noticed.

I had become so close to Ashley's family in the past year that I was invited to their Boxing Day party, which they reserved for their closest friends and relatives. I loved listening to her family speak, because they were from England and they had the most amazing accents. Once we even made tape recordings of her grandmother as she watched Ricki Lake. A bunch of gangsters were fighting, and Ashley and I almost peed in our pants when she said, "Look at them getting into a scruffy dog-and-cat fight."

Of course, the language thing could cut the other way, too. I used a lot of phrases that were different from theirs. Once I described someone as having a lot of spunk in front of Ashley's English friends. They were horrified because the word means sperm in England.

There was no language barrier of any sort when I finally decided that I had to tell someone about Mark.

It happened during a sleep-over at Ashley's house after swimming. We were eating ice cream and drinking Diet Coke in bed with the lights out. At the time Ashley had a crush on a boy named John. She had just finished talking about him when she asked, "Do you have a crush on anyone, Katie?"

I thought it would be better not to get into the Mark situation. But I didn't feel like I was lying, either; I mean, Mark wasn't a crush, it was deeper.

"No," I said as I grabbed the can of Diet Coke and placed it on the white carpet.

"No, not at all," she said, mocking me in her half-British accent.

"No, but I am talking to someone on AOL."

"You are not. How weird is that, Katie?"

"No, it isn't, we've been talking since September."

"Who is he? Where is he from?"

"He's from California, near Los Angeles. And he's *twenty-three.*"

"*Twenty-three?*"

"Yes."

"Katie, he just wants to talk to you about sex."

"No, actually we don't ever really talk about sex."

"So you don't have cybersex with him?"

"Ashley, don't be gross. You know me better than that."

"I thought I did, but I guess I didn't."

The Internet was still new to most people. Ashley knew about AOL, she even had her own account. But she didn't really try to talk to people on the Net.

"Ashley, he's a really great guy, really intelligent." I was beginning to regret telling her. "He's very caring and sensitive. Some guys are, you know. Maybe not the boys we know, but real guys can be."

"Katie, he just wants to talk about sex with you. He's just feeding you this bullshit now so that later he can get into all kinds of gross stuff and you'll accept it. What's his screen name, anyway?"

"Vallleyguy, with three l's."

"What a freak."

"No he isn't, not at all."

Ashley dropped the topic, and I didn't say a word more. I knew she wasn't going to be able to understand the nature of our relationship.

Ashley had proved to me that no one else would be able to understand either. Besides, Mark had recently told me that he was not twenty-three but rather thirty-one. I didn't get upset about this, because by now I couldn't imagine letting him go. But it would make the age difference even more dramatic in the eyes of others. I decided again that secrecy would be the best policy.

Something about the secrecy was seductive. There was a certain kind of power, control, even romance in knowing that together we were building our own relationship that no one else could influence, control, or even see. I just assumed that Mark hadn't told anyone about our relationship. As far as I knew, he didn't have much family. And I also assumed that any friends he had he had made through business, so I didn't think he really had anyone to tell either.

Of course, I was a little embarrassed by it all. I mean, Internet relationships are not exactly something that people respect. I know that my sister Abby believes it is like giving up on real life. And she has serious doubts about any guy who is looking for someone on the Internet. Why would any normal guy spend his time surfing the Net instead of going out in person to meet people? But I was using the Internet to meet people, too. I had to imagine that Mark was like me, a regular person who was looking for someone special.

>>>

As we got closer, Mark seemed to worry more and more about our secret being found out. Over and over again he wrote, "You really wouldn't want your mother finding out about this."

I didn't need him to tell me this. I had never considered telling my parents. The only way they would ever know about Mark, I thought, was if we were still together when I was eighteen.

We had a very complicated relationship. One minute we might talk about kid stuff—like making snowmen—and the next we'd be in a deep political debate. At fourteen I was a Republican because my parents were, and I liked to think I knew everything about politics. I was cocky about it, especially with my friends, but maybe even with Mark.

Mark was a political independent. He said that people who tied themselves down to one party were complete idiots. He had voted for Clinton, and was proud of it. He said that he blamed Reagan for all our national debt problems. He thought most Republicans would tar and feather him for that comment, but he didn't really care.

In the middle of all our chatting about everything under the sun, I told Mark about how I was training for the junior nationals in swimming, which were to be held in Texas. I was also preparing for a piano competition, and I had tons of rehearsals for my choir, which was to sing at the all-state convention. Even if Mark came to Connecticut, I wouldn't be able to see him very much.

Mark couldn't have been more sympathetic. "I'd do anything in the world for you, Katie," he said. "I have the money to buy you almost anything, you know. The sky's the limit."

"Mark, I don't need anything like that, you know."

"Then how about if I come to see you? How would you like that?"

That evening I had the house to myself. I had just carried the portable phone into the living room and what he said made me stop in my tracks.

"I'd really like to see you face-to-face. It would be so much better than being on-line or on the phone. I'd make you laugh. You know I would."

I sat down on the piano bench and stroked a couple of notes. He kept talking.

"You're at the piano? Could you play something for me? How about 'Ode to Joy' or 'Chopsticks'?"

"Mark, those are first-year pieces. You must have heard them a million times."

"That's okay. I want to hear them. I want to hear them as you would play them."

"All right then, I guess."

I played the pieces he wanted, and a couple more. He listened quietly for a moment, then started talking over the music.

"What kind of piano do you have?"

"An old Baldwin."

"I once had a Yamaha. I think those are really great pianos, maybe even better than Steinway or . . . what's that German-sounding one?"

"Bösendorfer?"

"Yeah, they're just as good as Bösendorfer. I once had a Yamaha, a white baby grand."

"That's so tacky," I teased. "You might as well own a red one or a pink one."

"Play some more."

He was silent for a moment while I played. I finished a short piece, and in half of a beat he spoke.

"What if I came to Texas?"

At first, I didn't know what to say.

"Katie, what if I were to fly there from California so we could meet?"

"Oh, I'm not sure it's the right time or place. It's a national meet, you know. I'm going to be under a lot of pressure."

"Katie, are we ever going to get together?"

"What do you mean?"

"Are we just going to talk forever? This has been going on for six months, you know. I thought we had a connection, that you wanted to see me as much as I want to see you."

"But I do . . ."

"All right, then you're probably just nervous. That's understandable. But believe me, it's okay. I'm just going to come, and I'll see you there. Even if it's just an hour, that's okay. We deserve it, don't you think?"

I couldn't answer.

"Katie? Do you want to see me?"

"Yes."

"All right then. It's settled. I can't wait."

He asked if he should stay at the same hotel my team had booked. I said yes, but I told him I had never seen the place, so he should not expect much. I didn't know what kind of hotels he was used to staying in, or whether he knew how to rough it.

"There's probably going to be five hundred girls and their coaches in this hotel," I warned. "It could be really noisy."

"I can handle it, no problem. I really want to finally meet you."

"Me too."

>>>

The day before I left I was excited, as if it were Christmas Eve, or the day before my birthday. It was a Monday night. I didn't have to swim that day, because they rarely made us swim before a large meet.

So after doing a little homework, I began to lay some clothes out on my bed. My family always says I overpack. I am not quite as bad as David, who once packed seven shirts for two days, but I can overdo it. This time I had an excuse. The winter climate in Dallas is iffy. It could be cold or warm. It could rain or be perfectly sunny. That meant I had to bring many types of clothing, because I always felt it was better to be safe than sorry.

Eventually, the wardrobe I chose covered my bed, and that didn't include shoes. I packed jeans, sweaters, shorts, dresses, you name it, I had it in there. I wanted to have choices when I got to Texas. And though I do think about my clothes a lot, I honestly didn't think about what I would wear when I first met Mark. I knew that given the way he felt about me, anything—even jeans and a T-shirt—would be fine.

It was about ten P.M. when Mark called. I was excited to hear his voice. In my mind he was no longer just an on-line buddy that I met in a chat room. He had become the love of my life. I loved the way he talked. It was soothing and sweet. I lay back on my bed, feeling comfortable, happy, *loved*.

"Yup, I'm just about ready to go," I told him. "I've got a little packing to do, and some homework to finish."

"I've got my ticket," he said.

I could hear a clothes dryer running in the background. Mark said he was doing some laundry before leaving.

"I've never washed my own clothes, ever," I told him.

"You've got to be kidding. What kind of spoiled brat are you?"

"Hey, I'm only fourteen. Besides, we've always had someone to do these things."

"I'm kidding you, Katie."

"It's kind of cute, you doing the wash like that."

"I know how to cook, too. Everybody should have these kinds of basic skills, Katie. It's part of life."

At that moment I thought I heard a woman's voice in the background wherever Mark was. "Hold on," he said, and he covered the phone with his hand. When he came back on the line he chuckled and then said, "I'm sorry."

"Who was that?" I asked.

"Oh, just my sister-in-law. She's visiting," he said.

I couldn't remember him ever saying he had a brother, but I let this pass.

We avoided talking about how meeting would change our relationship. As much as I wanted to see Mark, there was a part of me (a very small part) that wanted to just have the voice and the image of him in that picture from Disney World. Meeting him would mean I would be forced to accept the way he really was, including whatever flaws I might see. I was sure I could do this, though. I mean, I knew what he looked like, and that was not what I was in love with.

"When I get to Dallas, I'm going to want to see you as soon as possible," he said.

"I don't know where I'll be, but you can leave a message on the hotel phone."

"Will you have your own room?"

"Ashley and I are sharing. It should be registered under my name, though."

"I want to spend as much time as possible with you. There's so much I want to ask, and I have a lot to tell you about myself, too. It'll be so much better, face-to-face."

"I gotta go Mark. It's late and I'm going to have trouble falling asleep as it is."

"I know, I'm really excited, too."

"Wow. I guess I'll see you tomorrow."

"Sweet dreams, Katie."

I hung up the phone and smiled to myself. I turned my head on my pillow, pulled my quilt up, and thought about him. Though I didn't expect it, I quickly fell asleep.

Together

>>>

Since I didn't have to leave until one in the afternoon, I went to my choral practice at 6:45 A.M. I joined the group, stood up tall, and opened my mouth, but my heart and mind were not in it. The same was true when I sat down at the piano to play an accompaniment.

I wasn't required to go to class after choir, so my mom took me to the hairdresser's for a trim. The haircutter was a young man named Daniel, who always wore black leather pants. He described my cut as "fun and flirtatious." When I left, he said, "See you in Hollywood, sexy!"

On the way home in the car I worried about meeting Mark. I was not concerned about whether I would seem smart enough, but I was worried about whether I would be attractive enough. I wasn't interested in seducing him, but I wanted to impress him. Would his face show that he was pleased to see me or disappointed?

When I got home my mom came upstairs with me to check my packing. I had a large bag stuffed with team towels, uniforms, and suits. I had another big rolling suitcase for all my other clothes. When my mother looked inside she said it was jammed with far too many things. She made me take out two shirts, a pair of jeans, and a sweater. "It would be all right if you just packed swimsuits," she said. "Because that's all you'll need. You're not going anywhere but the pool."

Soon after, we wrestled everything downstairs and into our family's green minivan. My mom drove and we stopped to pick up Ashley, her mother, and Elizabeth, another friend from the team.

The trip to Newark Airport took us through the Bronx, over the George Washington Bridge, and down the New Jersey Turnpike. For a while we tried to find every letter of the alphabet, in order, on the passing billboards. When we got tired of this we sang songs, including "Turkey in the Straw" and "Deep in the Heart of Texas." In the quiet moments, I imagined Mark going to the airport in Los Angeles and boarding a plane to see me.

As we drove around the airport, parked, and headed for the plane, I felt more and more excited about my decision to see Mark. I'm not sure whether everyone else thought I was anxious about the meet, or nervous about the trip, but my anticipation must have been obvious. My heart was filled with excitement. At last Mark and I were going to meet.

>>>

After the plane landed at the Dallas–Fort Worth airport, we found our luggage and dragged it to the yellow-and-black Hertz rental car counter. For a while, none of the clerks could find our reservation. While we waited, Ashley and I sat on the luggage and tried to spot "Texas big hair." My mother said that they probably have stations—like gas stations—where Texan women fill up with hair spray. It doesn't surprise me that Texas is a beauty pageant mecca. Even in the airport you can see that women invest a lot of time on their hair, makeup, and splashy clothes. Texas just feels different from Yankee country, in a way that I liked. Everything seemed so proper and friendly, and I loved the accents.

Ashley and I spent much of the car ride to the hotel, which wasn't far, trying to imitate Texan accents. Ashley would say something like "Yee-Haaah," and I'd shout, "Ride 'em, cowboy!" We probably sounded ridiculous.

We arrived at the Harvey Hotel around midafternoon. Our team filled the marble lobby in front of the counter. Other teams were also registering at the hotel, but I didn't recognize any of the girls. As our coaches and parents checked in, Ashley and I went to the gift shop, where we found a postcard picturing a man opening a trench coat in front of a busload of tourists. Written at the top were the words "Everything's big in Texas." We laughed, and Ashley even bought one. You certainly didn't find postcards like that in Connecticut.

Mark wasn't supposed to arrive until around seven o'clock that evening. But as I walked through the hotel I wondered if any of the people in the lobby could be him. I had seen a picture of him, but I didn't think I would be able to recognize him in the crowd.

Ashley and I shared a room with two double beds. It was an average hotel room, except for the Bibles. There were four sitting in the nightstand. There were so many that at first I thought they were phone books. Then I thought that people in Texas must have an awful lot to pray about.

That night we were meeting downstairs for a quick meal before bed. I sat at a table with Ashley and Elizabeth. My mother, the coaches, and the rest of the parents sat away from us. I was so nervous I could hardly eat my pasta. When the waitress saw this, she teased me. "Are you sure you can't finish, Missy?" she said as she placed her hand on her hip. "You know your little body is going to need some more fuel than that." That was impossible, but Ashley and Elizabeth both ordered ice cream. I was so anxious I couldn't even look at it.

After the waitress walked away I checked my watch and noticed that it was already a little after seven. It made me nervous knowing that at any time Mark could walk through, and my mother was sitting nearby. But I kept pretending nothing special was about to happen. It was simply a casual dinner, teammates loading up on pasta on the night before a meet.

As soon as the check was paid we went up to our rooms. I tried not to think about Mark's arrival. I tried to act normal so that the others wouldn't get suspicious. I began to think about whether I could really pull it off. Could a man fly halfway across the country and meet me in a strange hotel without anyone knowing? I quickly banished my doubts and focused instead on how I would do it.

In the hotel room I shared with Ashley I waited and waited without a word from Mark. I tried to watch TV to pass the time. I think it was a news show like *Dateline*, but I'm not sure now. I heard voices coming from the set and saw that there was some sort of picture, but that was all. I was lost in imagining Mark's voice, his words, and his face as the door to one of the hotel's rooms swung open.

By 8:45, which felt like 9:45 to me, I was convinced that he had changed his mind and was not coming. I was disappointed. I had thought about his arrival constantly for over twenty-four hours.

I was so sure that he wasn't coming that I decided to put on my pajamas and go to bed. Ashley wanted to go to sleep too, so we both got ready. While she went to the bathroom I changed into a white camisole, a white Gap T-shirt, and then my flannel polar bear pajamas. They were my favorite pajamas, a Christmas gift from my grandparents when

I was in the fifth grade. Because I had worn them so much the flannel was rubbed smooth from wear, so smooth you couldn't even tell it was once flannel. There was a hole under one armpit and a hole in the left leg, but I still wore them. I loved them. Feeling cozy and safe in my familiar pajamas, I got under the covers, turned out the light, and rolled over to sleep. It was 9:15.

>>>

It was 9:37 when the phone rang. I mumbled a hello and the phone cord became tangled around my hand.

"Hello," he said, with a hint of excitement in his voice.

"I thought you weren't coming, why were you late?" I talked softly since Ashley was awake and in the bathroom.

"I missed my connection. Actually, it was pretty close. I was running through the airport and got to the gate just as the plane was leaving. There wasn't another flight for a couple of hours."

"Well, you're here now."

I sat up from the bed and leaned forward to the phone. I dangled my feet and curled the phone cord as it moved over them.

"So when am I going to get to see you?" asked Mark. "Can you come down now?"

"I guess I can come down for a quick hello."

"I'm on the ninth floor, room 938."

"I'm on the eleventh."

"Well, get yourself down here."

"Okay."

I hung up the phone, got out of bed, and stood there for a moment to think about what I was doing. I was in my pajamas. I knew I wouldn't look my best, but I didn't think he should care. We were friends. More than friends, actually. It shouldn't matter how I dressed.

An hour earlier my mother had left her raincoat in our room as she was going out to the grocery store to buy some breakfast food for the morning. Now that I was dashing out, I decided to grab the coat to cover my pajamas. As I did, Ashley came out of the bathroom.

"That was him, wasn't it?" said Ashley. "I knew he'd convince you to meet in person. He's here, isn't he?"

"We're just going to say hi. That's it."

"Katie, I don't think . . ."

"He's in 938. If you get worried, you can call me down there."

When I went to the door, Ashley jumped in front of me. I couldn't do anything else but laugh because I thought she was joking. But she insisted that I stay and braced herself with one hand on the door handle and the other pressed against the door frame.

"You can't go see this freak," she said. "I won't let you."

"He's not a freak. Let me out."

I knew she was just ignorant, unable to understand a mature relationship. I looked at her and tugged on the door. She was not going to stop me, and she knew it, so she let go. Neither of us said anything as the door swung closed behind me.

I paced the hall as I waited for an elevator. I couldn't imagine what was taking so long. There were six of them, after all. Then I heard the chime, which was not so different, I guess, from the chime that announces "You've got mail" on AOL. The door opened. I got inside and pressed the button. Nine. The doors closed, and I took a deep breath.

>>>

I stood outside Mark's door for a minute, looking at the PRIVACY PLEASE sign on the knob, steadying myself. I was now about to meet the man I loved. He knew so much about me, but also very little. He knew my stories, my struggles, and my accomplishments. But he knew none of the thousands of little things that become clear when people meet in person—every gesture, turn of the head, change in the voice. I felt strange, almost disoriented, and extremely nervous. I lifted my hand and tapped gently on the door.

I was expecting to meet a trim man, based on his photo, but when Mark opened the door I was absolutely shocked by how short he was. Since I am short, I always expect that people are the same height as I am, or taller. Mark was tiny. And he was the scrawniest man I had ever seen.

Later Mark would say he hugged me at the door, but I can't remember that. It could have happened, but I wouldn't bet money either way. He walked over to the sofa and invited me to join him there. Instead, I went to the chair that was facing him. I sat down and looked at him more carefully.

He was wearing dark jeans, the kind of deep blue denim that you expect to see on a cowboy, and a shirt with vertical stripes of maroon and cream against a blue background—navy blue to match the jeans.

I would have stopped thinking about how he looked if it hadn't been for the shoes. They were hideous. They were white canvas with a chunky rubber heel, very feminine. They might have been somewhat stylish for a girl at the time, but I couldn't imagine a man wearing them. I couldn't stop staring at his shoes, even after he started talking

"How was your trip?"

"Okay, okay." I couldn't think clearly enough to say anything more.

"God, I can't believe I missed that connecting flight. We

were late taking off, and then they circled the airport for what seemed like forever. The pilot said they would hold the planes for people with connections, but of course they didn't."

"Uh-huh."

"I'm hungry. Are you hungry? I haven't had anything all day, really. Why don't you just go up and put on some jeans and we can go out?" he said.

Go out? It was close to ten o'clock. I had to wake up at dawn. And besides, I was fourteen years old. There was no way I could just leave the hotel without someone knowing.

"Mark, I ate, and besides, it's pretty late, don't you think?"

"But there's no room service after ten, and I'm really starving."

I just looked at him and he finally gave in to the fact that I wouldn't go no matter what he said. I began to feel a little uncomfortable. Nervous.

"I've been in worse hotels," he said, suddenly changing the topic. "But they're pretty cheap here. I mean, come with me and look at this bathroom."

He got up, and so did I. He waited until I started moving and then placed his hand on my back to direct me. No one had ever steered me like that before. And with his touch I suddenly realized how uncomfortable I felt with him.

This wasn't at all what I had expected. We were such good friends—more than friends—on the Internet. No one had ever made me feel safer and more at ease. But here, in his presence, I was anxious and confused.

"Look at this," Mark said once we were in the bathroom. "There's not even a soap dish, and the towels are so thin they might as well be made of paper."

I couldn't look Mark in the eye; in fact, I couldn't look

at him at all. I glanced into the large mirror that was behind the sink instead, and felt a shiver of surprise to see my reflection joined by his. Then I gazed down at all the toiletries on the counter. He had a large silver can of Gillette shaving cream, which seemed awkward to me. He also had a large bottle of cologne.

"Smell this," he said. He picked it up and waved it under my nose.

"Yuck, Mark. I can't stand the smell of cologne."

"Katie, just stand still," he said. He put his hands on my shoulders and then looked past me into the mirror. "I thought you would be taller."

I wanted to say to him that I thought he would be a lot taller himself. But I didn't. "Well, I told you I was short" was all I could mutter.

Mark wanted to show me a new watch that he had bought and he rushed out of the room to get it. I followed him and he gave it to me to hold. The weight and the quality made me think it was solid gold.

"Is it real, I mean, solid gold?"

"Of course. How could you even ask?"

He grabbed my hand to admire my own Seiko watch. As he did, he glimpsed my necklace. It was a fourteen-karat gold necklace with a piece of jade that was carved into the Buddha of laughter. He took the Buddha in his hand.

"This is beautiful, Katie. I really like it."

"My grandmother gave it to me. She brought it back from Thailand."

"I love your shoes, too."

They were simple Birkenstocks, the most common style sold, in the most common color.

"And your eyes . . . so pretty."

Mark stepped a little closer, looked into my eyes, and

then gently touched my shoulders, my waist. No grown man had ever inspected me like this before, and it made me self-conscious. I was glad that my pajamas covered me so well. I nervously played with my necklace. He sat down on the sofa. I stood for a moment, then glanced at the television.

"Do you think it's possible to get a VCR in this hotel?" I asked. "Ashley and I brought some videos."

"You could probably rent one," he said, then added quickly, "Come sit here on the sofa."

Without thinking, I did what he said and sat down on the opposite end of the sofa, facing him.

"I need a haircut," he said.

"No, you don't," I said. He seemed feminine, worrying so much about his hair.

"Give me your hand," he said. "I can read your fortune."

I played along, giving him my right hand. He turned it over so he could examine the lines that hold the answers to life's mysteries. He began to stroke the life line.

"I can see right here that you are going to have a long, rich life."

He continued to caress my hand. It felt comforting. But when I tried to pull back, he held on harder. It became more difficult to concentrate on what we were supposed to be talking about because my attention was fixed on his hands touching mine. There was a strength in his hands that was different from mine. His skin was smooth. The small lines seemed more defined, and the hair on the back of his hands was more conspicuous.

I had never felt a man's hand in this way. I never held David's hand. And it had been years since my grandfather had stopped taking my hand, the way grandfathers take the hands of their little granddaughters.

"Katie, I have been thinking about you all day," he said softly. "And I have been thinking about doing this."

This. I knew what "this" was. I knew he wanted to kiss me. I felt a shiver of anxiety, not because I didn't want him to, but because I was so inexperienced.

I didn't move as he leaned forward. I closed my eyes and could feel the warmth of his face as it came close. I wanted to be a good kisser. Not because it was expected of me. Not because I was swept up in passion. I wanted it because of what I felt for Mark, and because I didn't want to say no.

Our lips met and I felt his tongue slip under mine. It was fat, and wet, and warm. I felt a few stray whiskers that he had missed with the razor, and suddenly I realized that this was a grown man who was giving me my first real kiss, not a fuzzy-faced teenager, not someone my own age.

Something inside me snapped. Now I didn't want this at all. But I couldn't speak. I hesitantly pulled away. He lifted my shirt and grabbed my breast. Now the strength of his hands meant something different. It hurt, but I said nothing. I felt completely numb. And then I thought, Do I owe this to Mark?

"C'mon sweetie, relax."

He tried to reach into my pajama bottoms through the fly opening. I pulled his hand away. He did it again, and I pulled his hand away again. Then he pushed down on me hard, letting me know he would not be resisted again.

Instead of being angry and shouting at him to stop it, I was confused and speechless. Mark was supposed to be better than this. He was supposed to be patient and kind and generous. He was supposed to care about me. Now it was clear that he obviously wanted me to have sex with him. That was what this meeting was about. He moved on top of me. I wondered what a mature person, a woman, would do, but I could think of nothing.

"We could have such a good future," he whispered.

"How do you know?"

"A little bird is telling me."

It was silly and I laughed nervously. It was then quiet, and I had a moment to think about how much I really cared about him.

"I love you," I said.

I told him because I wanted him to know how much I looked up to him. He was everything that I thought a person should be. And when he said nothing in response, I knew that I was wrong about him, about myself, about love, about everything.

>>>

The knocking on the door was so loud that it made me panic. I have never been so instantly frightened. It sounded as if a giant were pounding on the door.

Startled by the sound, we both sat up. The color drained from Mark's face. I knew, and I think he knew, too, who had to be on the other side of the door.

"Can I help you?" Mark called out.

"Is Katie Tarbox in there?"

The first thing I thought about was the disappointment I would see on my mother's face when the door opened. I didn't want her to know what I had done or who was in this room with me. How could I have put myself in this position? I thought. How could I jeopardize who I was and what I stood for this much?

Mark got up and walked over to the door.

"No, she's not here," he said.

My mother was not satisfied. "Has she been here at all tonight?"

We didn't know it at the time, but she was standing there with two of the team's coaches. One was about to leave to get the hotel security guard.

Mark looked at me, and the expression on his face asked, What should we do now? I hoped he would know what to do, but he didn't. Quickly and quietly we decided he would tell my mother that I had gone down to the lobby. When she left to go search for me, I would go back to my room. In the meantime, I would hide in the bathroom.

"She was here, but she left. She's downstairs."

"I want to come in to see for myself," my mother said.

Mark told her to come back in twenty minutes, after he "freshened up," and then she could search the room. My mother said she wasn't going anywhere. She would wait.

In the bathroom I looked at myself in the mirror. I saw my face and my pajamas, the same pajamas I had worn so many times in my own bed. I wondered how my mother was feeling. Mark opened the bathroom door and brought me out. I have never seen anyone so afraid.

"This hotel has security guards," he said under his breath. "This could get pretty out of control. You have to promise me that you won't tell what happened here tonight. You cannot tell anyone, not even your mother. I could get into a lot of trouble and I could even go to jail."

I thought to myself, I know this already. I really hate when people try to reaffirm things that I already know. It's incredibly condescending. I didn't promise him that I would keep quiet. But I didn't think he had to worry. I did not want to live with the guilt of turning him into some kind of criminal. How could he think I would do that? After all the times he'd been there for me, including my birthday, when nobody else could make it. Despite what had just happened I still loved him.

When Mark finally opened the door, we saw that my mother and the coaches had been joined by a security guard and two police officers, all of them male. No one said anything as I walked out, and I didn't dare look at my mother. I suddenly felt completely exhausted. I just wanted to go to bed. I walked down the hall past everyone. One of the swim coaches asked me where I was going. I stopped and turned, but I couldn't say anything.

Looking back, I saw Mark come out of his room. My eyes focused on his hideous white shoes. They were about the ugliest pair of shoes I had ever seen in my entire life.

He wanted to talk to my mother. She wanted nothing to do with him. He tried to convince my mother that nothing had happened, nothing at all. We just chatted, like good friends do. Nothing bad had happened.

I don't think my mom believed him. She walked down the hall, leaving Mark with the authorities.

I later learned that hotel security didn't come up at first when my mom went down to report that her child might be in danger. They said they would come to the room only if someone knew that I had been there, and they didn't come up until she sent two of the coaches down to confirm to them that I had been in the room.

No one said a word in the elevator. My mother was too upset. I didn't know what to say. The elevator stopped and my coaches left. I then went to my room with my mom. Once inside I got into the bed. I just wanted to sleep, but she didn't understand this at all. I was so confused. So much had happened in the last hour. I needed to be alone to think about who Mark really was, who I was, how this could have happened.

The Dallas police knocked on my mother's door about twenty minutes later. She let them in, and she told me that they had to take a report when these things happen. I condensed my story into three minutes at most. I told them that I had met Mark over the Internet. Then I said, "He came here. I went to his room. My mom found us. Nothing happened."

I didn't want to talk, and I knew that my mother was not ready to hear the truth. I knew that because I know my mother better than anyone else does.

Over and over they asked, "Are you sure nothing happened?"

My mom said she would leave the room if I wanted. I said it wasn't necessary. But I wasn't going to talk that night. Then another police officer came into the room. He asked me how old I thought Mark was and I told him thirty-one. He then asked me my age, and I told him fourteen.

"Miss, he is forty-one and he thinks you are fifteen."

I couldn't believe it. I just could not believe that Mark was that old. He could easily be my father. And I was certain that he knew my age. He had known from the beginning. How could he lie like that?

The officers asked me about his job. I told him I thought he owned some type of consulting firm. I didn't really know. He never really talked with me about his work. The police officer told me Mark was a financial consultant and he described his investment fund.

Then they asked if I knew where he lived. I said Woodland Hills, because that is what he told me. In fact, they said, Mark resided in Calabasas, California.

Finally they asked me his name. It seemed like a ridiculous question. "It's Mark," I said.

"No, it's not," they said. "His real name is Francis John Kufrovich."

We sat in silence for a moment. Then one of the police officers began to speak. "Let me get this straight, ma'am," he said. "I have spoken with this man for five minutes and I know his age, name, occupation, and residence. You have spoken with him for six months and don't know any of this?"

I realized, at that moment, that if Mark couldn't tell me the truth about these basic issues, then why should I believe anything he said? I said to the police officer, "No, I don't know these things. I'm sorry."

He didn't want me to be sorry but thankful that I had made it out of that room alive. This was a ridiculous statement. Based on our Internet conversations, I didn't have any reason to believe that Mark would harm me. I had heard all the horror stories of girls just like me who had been killed, chopped up into pieces, and buried by twisted psychopaths. But Mark, or Frank, or whatever his name was, couldn't be like that. He had been a good person to me. I had known him for six months, and he had never given me any solid reason not to trust him or to doubt his integrity.

My mom walked the police officers out, and I just lay under the covers. I looked out the windows and I wondered what I would do. I also wondered what was real about my Internet relationship with that man. Why didn't I suspect problems earlier? Why had I trusted him? Why had he lied to me? Who was that person in the hotel room?

My mom came back into the room and closed the door. She began to cry. She picked up the phone and called David. Her words were broken by sobs and almost incoherent. About all I could understand was that she had never been so mortified in her entire life. I had never seen her this upset.

My mom hung up the phone, and I tried to go to sleep. It was very difficult. I tried everything, but somehow counting sheep, or anything else, wasn't working. I knew I had to sleep, though, because the next morning I had to be in the pool. Through the whole, long, dark night I lay there, half-asleep, half-awake, numb, and in shock.

At about three in the morning, my mom got into bed with me. She just came over and wrapped her arms around me. I knew she was hurt very badly, and it was only then that I could sense the pain I had caused her. She kissed my cheek. She smelled my hair. At that moment, I knew she really loved me, and I just wanted to make everything right again.

In the morning I felt even more distraught than I had the night before. To make matters worse, my mom had bought bagels and cereal the night before for a team breakfast in our room. While it was still dark outside, the entire team filed in to eat. It was so early that no one was completely awake. But the silence, a kind of silence I hate, was caused by something more than sleepiness. Some people refer to it as an "elephant in the room." I guess that is the best phrase to describe it. Everyone knew what had happened, and no one said a word about it.

My mom tried to start a conversation. She said, "Aren't these bagels fresh?" or something like that. They were horrible bagels—stale and tasteless. No one answered my mother, and the tension in the room grew.

I really didn't have any appetite, but because I was going to have to swim for so many hours, my mom forced me to eat. I took a bite out of my bagel—to make it look like I was eating—and then put it down.

When the head coach walked in, she announced that she had had a long night. Then she said that we would have a team meeting that afternoon. The "incident" was going to be discussed, and everyone would get a chance to talk about its effect on the team.

It was hard to believe she said this. Nothing had happened to the team. It had happened to me. But somehow it involved my mother, my coaches, hotel security, the police, and now even my swim team. I was the one who was directly involved, but no one seemed to notice this or care much at all about how I was feeling.

>>>

After a silent ride to the pool, we all went inside, changed, and hopped in the water. Slowly, we began to swim in single file. The coaches went off somewhere, trusting us to warm up on our own. The comments began.

"Katie, I heard you slept with a fifty-year-old last night."

"Nothing happened, nothing at all," I snapped.

We were supposed to be concentrating on our swimming. Instead, my teammates wanted to know who Mark was, how long I had known him, how he had wound up in Texas, and what exactly had happened in his room, anyway?

While Ashley deflected their questions, I pulled myself out of the water and sat on the side waiting for my coaches to come back. Out of habit, I studied my feet. I loved the look of my pruned feet. It was proof of my long, hard work at the pool. I traced the ridges on my soles with my hands. For a moment I felt soothed, as I thought about the pool back home and what I had been doing before coming to this place. Then I felt sick to my stomach.

I don't throw up a lot, but I knew what was coming. I could feel the churning, so I ran to the bathroom and it just happened. It wasn't a lot. But the muscles in my stomach cramped hard, and it hurt.

At the sink I pulled off my swim cap and rubbed my

forehead gently, hoping to erase the red marks left from the cap and goggles. I looked up into the mirror to inspect the red depressions that circled my eyes. I never realized before what my emotions could do to my body. I began to brush my hair, attacking the knots. I thought, The only way this could get worse is if everyone finds out what actually happened in that room. I was the only one who really knew. And that fact gave me a little control over what was happening to me now. And standing before the mirror, I promised myself that I would never tell.

My mother walked into the bathroom and saw me sitting down. She brought me a muffin and water and forced me to eat. I shoved the muffin down my throat and took small sips of the water. She congratulated me on my swim and said that I was looking really good in the water that day. She said the week would be over soon, and that each event should come and go quickly.

She saw that I was distressed, but she couldn't know how angry I was feeling. I was in the middle of the most traumatic event in my life, and everyone—my mother included—had adopted a have-a-muffin, life-goes-on attitude. I missed school. I missed my home. I missed the me who existed before I went into Mark's room. And as much as I tried, I couldn't understand how this had happened to me.

My mother gave me a hug and told me it would be over soon.

I thought to myself, How can it be over soon? We still have five more days here, five more days to sit and think about what I experienced and what to do about it. She looked at me one more time, deep into my eyes, and asked if everything was fine.

I looked up at her, about to cry. I couldn't admit to what had happened. I couldn't tell her that her daughter, the girl

who always made her so proud, had made so many awful mistakes that led to what had happened last night. I had
to lie.

I wiped the tears from my eyes and told my mother
everything was fine. I had to be strong for her, because she
was already upset enough from last night. She blew me a kiss
as she walked out, saying she would see me later.

>>>

At the end of the day's competition I went to the locker
room and began packing my bag. Ashley walked in. "Good
swim," she told me as she pulled off her swim cap. I realized
that I was no longer looking at her through the same eyes.
Ashley may have been the same girl she always was, but I
was changed.

She walked by me into the shower. I looked up at her
from the bench and said something about seeing her at
dinner. She looked confused, and I worried that she, like
everyone else, was disappointed in me. I found it ironic that I
was looking up at her. I always thought that of the two of us,
I was the stronger one. I hadn't realized how weak I could be.

Here it was the first day after, and already I felt like I
just couldn't take it. I wanted to shout to the whole locker
room. I wanted to tell the truth. What had happened was
wrong. Covering it up was wrong, too. I wanted to confess
what Mark had done. But at the same time I felt compelled to
conceal the truth. I was embarrassed. Getting through each
hour was hard. How, I wondered, was I going to make it
through the rest of my life?

I asked myself this over and over and always came back
to the same answers. Telling would make everything more
real, and more awful. It could get Mark arrested and pull me
into a big investigation. I pictured court proceedings. Me testi-

fying. Mark going to jail. I just wanted it to go away. I wanted to wake up and discover it was all a terrible nightmare.

I got up and walked out of the locker room, down a hallway and then outside. The swim center was set in the middle of a grassy field, far from any houses or other buildings. Ashley joined me and we sat on the curb, waiting for our mothers to pick us up. She tried to tell me everything was going to be okay and I said, "No, it's not going to be okay at all." I kept trying to measure the amount of pain I would face if I told the truth, comparing it with the burden to do what was right.

When the car came, Ashley grasped my hands and lifted me off the sidewalk. She wrapped her arms around me and told me everything was going to be okay. How was it going to be okay? I had to choose between hurting someone I thought I cared about and doing what was right.

>>>

Back at the hotel, everyone assembled in one of the rooms for the promised team meeting. I found a place on the corner of one of the beds. My mother sat behind me, in one of the two chairs that were available. Most of the swimmers sat on the floor. Some of the parents stood in the corridor between the bathroom and the room. It was hot and claustrophobic.

The first one to speak was one of the younger coaches. Just out of graduate school at the University of Connecticut, she had red hair and fair skin to match. She wore glasses that always slid down her nose too much, which forced her to peer out at you over the rims in a way that made her seem condescending.

"As many of you already know, there was an incident involving Katie Tarbox last night."

As she said this the room seemed to get smaller. It definitely felt hotter, stuffier.

"Obviously we're at a national meet and what Katie has done, if people find out about it, will affect our team's reputation across the country," she continued. Everyone looked at me.

"Some swimmers on other teams already know that a New Canaan girl was missing last night." She told us we all had to assume that this couldn't be kept secret, but obviously she wanted us to try.

"This was completely unacceptable behavior," she said, looking directly at me. "And if Katie's mother wasn't here, she would have been flown home immediately." She paused for a long moment and stared at me again. "I think it would be appropriate for you to apologize to everyone here. We're all affected by what you have done."

There was silence. I looked to my mother and she didn't say anything. She didn't even move. A flash-fever of rage surged through me. I didn't want to apologize. I wanted to slap both of them, the coach and my mother.

What was I supposed to apologize for? Maybe I had put the reputation of our team on the line, whatever that meant, but I couldn't understand what they needed to hear from me. None of them knew what I was going through. And apologizing to them would just put the blame on me even more. Everyone was saying it was all my fault and no one else's. What about the man who was now on his way home to California? Why wasn't it his fault, too?

I rose slowly and just said, "I'm sorry."

No one said anything. In the silence, I cleared my throat and struggled to say something more. "I know I have made a huge mistake. I'm sorry that we had to have this team meeting. I'm sorry if this hurts the team or makes it hard for any of you to swim."

I stopped speaking. Still no one said a word. Then one of the mothers in the room began to cry.

"Maybe some of us, us adults, have some responsibility here, too," she said. "We didn't watch the girls enough. Maybe we gave them too much freedom." Everyone in the room began to grumble.

My mother didn't want to hear this, and she spoke up loudly. "No, it is Katie's fault and not the fault of the chaperones here," she insisted. "We have to place trust in the swimmers if we are going to compete at national meets. Katie should have known better, and it is not the parents' fault."

I felt bad that I had caused all this commotion, but I didn't understand why it was so serious to everyone else, when the incident had involved me. They weren't in that room with Mark. They didn't have his hands all over them. They weren't interrogated by the police or confronted with the possibility that the truth would send a man they loved to prison.

When it was over, my mom and I walked back to her room. She said, "Katie, we have a serious problem. I just don't know what we are going to do with you. You have been lying to us for so many months, and now you have involved the swim team and the police. I'm afraid we are going to have to seek outside help because I just can't help you anymore."

Was I really some sort of pathological liar? Was not telling them everything about my life really lying? Didn't I have the right to some privacy?

>>>

The next morning my mom went down early to get a table for breakfast. Shortly after, I walked downstairs. I sat down with a big bowl of strawberries. They were fresh and juicy. One packet of sugar made them perfect. For a moment, for the first time in two days, I felt at ease.

"Why, Katie? Why did you have to do this?"

"I wish I knew the answer."

"Do you think it would be appropriate if David dated Karen?"

"No, but I never thought he was that old."

"Why did you even bother with him? That's what I'd like to know."

"He was someone to talk to, Mom," I said as I ate more strawberries. "You haven't been around a lot with all your business trips and the fact that you live at work doesn't help."

My mom doesn't like it when other people are right, and by the look on her face I could see I may have been right about this. She knew she hadn't been around much. In fact, she had been away for my birthday that year. "I think that you think it was neat that you were able to get the attention of an older person," she said. "Do your friends know about this?"

This conversation was going nowhere. She knew that Ashley was the only one who really knew the details. What good would it do to go over that ground again? Besides, there was no way that I would admit to myself that my relationship with Mark was wrong. And she wasn't going to look at the fact that she had been absent from my life for a long time.

We wouldn't really try to talk again for the rest of the meet. Looking back at it now, I can see that in the cold silence I was in a state of either shock or depression. All I knew then was that the days seemed endless. It became more and more difficult to face my mother, my swim coaches, and my teammates. Each one of them knew I wasn't feeling myself, and lying to them hurt me even more. I would walk by Ashley at times and I just couldn't find the right words to say to her. All I really wanted to do was escape from everyone and spend some time thinking about something else, feeling something other than sorrow and shame.

At times I felt ready to tell the whole truth about what had happened. I would get up the courage and then look at my mother and feel completely intimidated.

When I was alone, I questioned everything I once took for granted about myself. I had always thought I was an intelligent, thoughtful, moral person, especially compared with other kids. But the worst thing friends my age were doing was drinking. I had had serious romantic feelings for a much older man. I wondered if I would ever be forgiven, or if I would ever be able to forgive myself.

When the last day of the meet finally came, I felt relieved knowing I wouldn't ever have to go to this pool again. In the locker room I struggled out of my lucky socks. I had worn them for important events since I was five years old, and they fit like a second skin. I stretched my swimsuit over my body. This was a struggle, too, because the suit was four sizes too small. I often have trouble choosing suits. At a previous meet, I swam in a large one, and my breasts almost fell out. This time I opted for a small one, to be safe. But the back straps dug into my skin, and the fabric rubbed against a rash that had broken out all over my body.

My feet hurt, too, as I walked out onto the bars of the pool bulkhead. I stood beside my lane and jumped up and down a little to warm my muscles. For a minute my mind flashed on my recurring nightmare of being naked and exposed. I forced this thought out of my head and looked at my mom in the stands. I smiled. She looked at me through a video camera.

I felt like I owed my team every ounce of effort I could give. I was conflicted about the charges against me, but I could admit that I had disrupted everyone's state of mind. The focus was no longer on swimming but on me. I had let them all down—the swimmers, the coaches, the parents—and I wanted to redeem myself. I didn't want to make this trip a complete failure.

The whistle blew, which signaled that it was okay to enter the water for warm-ups. My mind seemed to switch back and forth from the pool and the swim ahead to how much I had let everyone down. I just wanted them to think I was a good person again.

When the race began, I strained to make a perfect flying start. My legs slammed the water hard and I threw myself into the butterfly. In the water, the voices that echoed off the concrete walls and the pool deck were muffled to a soft, gurgly murmur. I swam hard, thankful for the solitude. But in all my straining to swim fast, I forgot to take a breath. I didn't swim well at all. I was lucky to even finish.

When it was over and I got out of the pool, I just sat down and cried. One of the coaches came over to me. "You're just hyperventilating," she said. "Try to calm yourself. Breathe slowly." I wasn't hyperventilating. I was falling apart.

When I was able to get control of myself, I got up and slipped into the locker room. There I put on some flip-flops and shorts and I went outside. It was quiet. Not another soul was anywhere to be seen. I looked out over the grass field and just started walking.

I went up the slope of a hill to a field where I sat down and played with the grass. Like a little girl, I twisted blades into necklaces and crowns. I thought about what had happened, and how Mark, my mother, and I might each see this situation. Was I really protecting Mark by hiding the truth? How could I continue to lie to my mother? Would anyone even believe me now if I told?

Ashley walked up the hill and asked what I was doing. I wasn't too sure. Without much conviction I said I needed to be alone. She suggested that we roll down the hill together. It was a funny suggestion. I hadn't done something like that in years. But I liked the idea of doing something, anything, other than worrying. So we lay down in the grass, folded our arms over our chests, and rolled down the hill, laughing as we reached the bottom.

>>>

My mom and I were in her hotel room together as we prepared to go out to dinner on our last night in Texas. She stood in the bathroom drying her hair. As I sat in a chair in the room waiting, I thought about that week, and I was amazed that I had gotten through it. I wondered what was going to happen when I got home. How would people treat me once they found out what had happened?

"Katie, you know David talked to the New Canaan police captain today," my mom said from the bathroom. "We are going to look into charging him for endangering the morals of a minor."

"Does this mean I'm going to have to talk to more police?" I asked as I sat in the chair looking down at my swimsuit.

"Yes, Katie, this is a very serious thing. Why don't you understand how serious it is?" she asked in a bitter tone.

I didn't think my encounter with Mark was that bad; in fact, I was convinced that my parents were not good people for not understanding or trusting me.

"Mom, will I have to tell them what happened in the room?" I asked softly, trying to say it so she couldn't hear it with her hair dryer on.

"What did you say, Katie?" She turned off the dryer and came out.

"Mom, I have to come clean," I said. I didn't cry, but I was weeping inside as I told her that Mark had touched me when we were alone. I described how he put his hands inside my shirt and how he went for my crotch. It was a hard thing to do. I knew that telling her meant that the whole thing was going to get worse, not better. But I couldn't lie any longer.

"I am so sorry, Mom. Please forgive me. I know I'm a bad person. Just please forgive me."

My mom looked me in the eye with the kind of stern look that you never want to get because you know you are in really deep, deep shit.

"How am I supposed to believe you now when all you have done is lie for over six months? This could ruin a man's life, Katie. Do you understand? This is not some joking matter. I don't know why I am supposed to believe you now. How can I? Who is going to believe a word you say after you lied about it the other night?" She was screaming at me.

I understood that I had lied, but I had just done the hardest thing in my entire life. Of course I understood what the truth could do to Mark. That's why it took me so long to tell.

"Mom, you just have to believe me. I swear. You just have to believe. Just this once, can you please believe me?"

"I thought you guys drank a Coke in the room. That's what he told me," my mom answered.

"I would never drink a sugar soda. You know that," I said to her.

"So you would lie to me, police officers, and your team,

but you wouldn't drink a sugar soda? Some morals you have, Katie," she snapped back at me.

I couldn't say anything. My mom sat down on the bed and pulled out the number for the police officers. "I'm going to call the police, Katie. Are you sure this is the truth?"

"Yes, it is." I still kept my head bowed. My mom dialed the phone number very slowly, hitting each number on the keypad very hard. The officers said they would come over that night, before I went home, to make a report.

"Now we're not going to get to go out tonight. I hope this makes you happy, Katie. All because of you, no one is going to be able to go out to dinner," my mom yelled at me.

I couldn't forgive myself for all of the pain and anguish I was causing her. These things weren't supposed to happen to families like mine. My mom left the room and I overheard her tell my coach, "I'm sorry, but we won't be able to go out tonight. Apparently, there is a little bit more to the story." She also went to Ashley's mom and told them we would be unable to drive them to dinner. Ashley and her mother decided to stay, and they told us that they would meet us downstairs for a late meal. It was nice to know that I had some support.

When the two policewomen arrived, my mom apologized for calling them again. She felt that it would be better if she left the room during the interview. That way I wouldn't feel pressured by her presence. I was kind of sick of seeing her, to be honest. She obviously didn't understand what I was going through, and she was placing all of the anger that she had for Mark on me.

Since neither of the policewomen were there the night of the incident, they knew very few of the original details. Once again I had to describe how I met Mark, why he was in Texas, and why I was there. As I spoke, I kept looking at their badges. I felt like a criminal.

"Can you please describe as vividly as you can, Miss, what happened in the room that night?"

That was the question I dreaded the most. I closed my eyes to picture what had happened. It all came back to me, in surprising detail, and this time I didn't leave anything out in the telling. I included how I had met him over the Internet, how the relationship had grown over six months, how we planned to meet in Texas, and every detail of how he had touched me and where. I knew I was doing the right thing, but I was confused about why. I knew Mark was going to find out, that he could be in very big trouble. I felt bad for him and embarrassed for myself.

I was glad when I got to the part when my mom knocked on the door, because they knew the story after that. I was done. It was now on the record that Mark had done those things to me. I can't tell you how relieved I felt, and for a moment I thought that maybe I could be a good person. Yes, I had made mistakes—many—but I was trying to correct them.

My mom and I thanked the police officers and they told us they would be in touch. Again they told me I was extremely lucky to be alive. Girls who got hurt were different from me, I thought. They prowled the streets at night, courting trouble. I couldn't accept that I was anything like that, or that Mark could be dangerous in that way.

When they finally left it was 9:30, and we were both very hungry. Ashley and her mom were downstairs waiting for us to order. For the first time since my mother had knocked on the door to Mark's room I thought things might be okay. Ashley's mother tried to comfort me by telling me a story of a girl who had been raped on her block. In many ways she was trying to be helpful. She told me a little about the English judicial process. The story did nothing to make me feel better, but at least it changed the subject for a moment.

Our break was interrupted when the police officers walked into the restaurant and asked my mom if we were willing to press charges. My mom looked me in the eye and said, "What choice do we have? We will press charges. We have to."

I couldn't believe she hadn't even consulted me. She was so concerned with doing the right thing that she just automatically said yes. I only wish the police officers had explained to us what pressing charges meant. I wish they had said that it would involve FBI interviews, polygraph tests, court appearances, and much more. If they had, I would have known to be brave, to find the courage within me to continue and not be surprised by anything that would happen. I wish they had told me this was going to take the next two years of my life.

Slut

>>>

At first my parents and I had an understanding about life after Texas. I was going into counseling, even though I didn't want it, but aside from that, we were going to hold on to our normal lives as hard as we could. I wouldn't be missing any school. They would go to work, and hopefully the normal routine would ease some of the shock and pain.

This was fine, in theory. But from the moment my relationship with Mark began, I had lived in dread that my friends and teachers would find out. My conversation with Ashley had confirmed my fear and the experience in Texas had made it worse. This wasn't some trivial thing like a fashion faux pas or a conflict with a classmate. I knew what this could do to my reputation. And though the girls on the swim team were supposed to keep things to themselves, I knew that was impossible. Gossip is irresistible, especially for teenage girls.

At home, I tried to live normally. My parents had not banned me from the Internet because I think they were sure I must have learned my lesson. For a while, when no one was around, I logged on and looked for a message from Mark. None ever came, and in a few weeks I stopped checking.

Both of my sisters judged me harshly. Carrie was extremely angry with me for disrupting our family. I had become the uncomfortable focal point of life in our house. Carrie was upset because she needed attention—regular old parental attention—and wasn't getting it. Unfortunately, understanding this didn't make her words any less painful to hear.

Abby was even more harsh than Carrie. She told me she was disappointed in me and was convinced that I was totally responsible for all that had happened. "It's not like you were just walking down the street and were molested," she said. "I'm really disgusted with you," she told me, over and over. "You've ruined our family. You've ruined our lives. I am so disappointed in you that it seems like I don't even know you."

>>>

On the night before I was supposed to go back to school I tossed and turned and just couldn't get comfortable. Even when I did fall asleep, I couldn't stay asleep. I would wake up and the dread would be right there, in my stomach, rising through my chest. I'd rush to the bathroom to vomit and then go back to bed.

I watched the minutes and hours pass on the clock until I could go to my mother's room to tell her that I had been throwing up all night and didn't think I could go to school. I wasn't prepared for what she said next.

"Katie, I never thought I would ask you this, but are you pregnant?"

I was mortified and offended. I couldn't believe she'd asked me that. I was outraged. There was no possible way I could be pregnant. I told her, and I thought she truly believed me.

I didn't go to school that day, though my parents went

in to meet with my guidance counselor. They were worried about my safety, afraid that Mark would come and take me away and try to hurt me. Their fear made me start to think that maybe Mark could be dangerous. Some small part of me began to see Mark as a threat. Without telling anyone why, I rearranged the furniture in my room until I was sure my bed couldn't be seen from the windows.

Freed from going to school, I was able to relax, but only for a while. I was scheduled to go to the New Canaan Police Department in the afternoon to answer some questions that had been sent by the officers in Texas. They were determined to continue the investigation and the New Canaan police were helping. They had also asked for photos of Mark, which I had, and copies of some of our e-mails. My parents weren't surprised that I had these things hidden in my room, but they weren't happy about it, either.

I was cooperating with the police because my parents wanted me to, but I was only pretending to agree that a serious crime had taken place. In my mind, Mark was still my best friend, the one I had trusted. And despite everything, I still wanted to trust him. What occurred in that hotel room lasted a few minutes. It didn't wipe out the last six months or everything we had together. I still wanted to call him up. I felt that we had experienced a trauma together and part of me—a stronger part than the part that saw him as a threat—felt that we could help each other out. It didn't matter to me that he had lied about everything. He had lied for a good reason: to protect our relationship. In a way, I loved him for that.

Abby took me to the police station, but we left early enough to stop at a Friendly's Ice Cream store for a Reese's Peanut Butter Cup sundae, but instead of making me feel better it only made me feel ill. At the police station I answered the questions—pretty basic stuff about how Mark and I met and became closer—and even though I was reluctant to hand them over, I left the pictures and e-mails.

When I was dealing with the police, it was hard to tell whether I was in trouble or not. No one actually said that I had committed any crime, but I was treated sternly, and I was never told that I was innocent.

Besides protecting myself, I was also careful to protect Mark. I didn't lie, but when I was pushed to make him seem like a predator, I resisted. I reminded them that most of the conversations Mark and I had had weren't sexual at all. And I told them that he had not physically hurt me in the hotel room. Though I thought the chances of him going to jail were slim, I didn't want it to happen at all. I had also been part of what happened in Texas. I was a mature person. I was just as responsible for this as he was. In cooperating with the police, I was playing a role—the good child—I had to play in order to be redeemed in my parents' eyes. But I wasn't going to sell Mark out.

If anything, I believed that I was being victimized more by how people were reacting to what had happened. The way I saw it, except for those few moments in the room, Mark had been good to me by telling me how smart I was or how I was a good person. But the police, my family, and my friends were all changing everything they thought about me. They were questioning my very identity, and making me question it, too. I wasn't Katie Tarbox, good girl. I was Katie Tarbox, slut, or idiot, or both.

>>>

Everyone seemed to have a visceral reaction to what I had done, and a label for me. "I am not going to let my child grow up and become a burden on society," my mother said. Though David never put it this way, I felt he decided I was mentally ill the moment he found out about Mark. He, more than my mother, insisted that I see a psychologist, and he set up a couple of appointments.

I didn't want to talk to more strangers. I didn't want therapy. I didn't want to bond. I also had a problem confronting the fact that I had fallen in love over the Internet. How did it happen? Why did it happen? I'm not sure that my parents wanted the answers to these questions any more than I did. But in seeking therapy, we were doing the right thing, the responsible thing.

Psychologist Number One was a lady in a dark navy blazer and skirt with a pastel shirt. She was thin, with short brown hair and a big smile that made her seem like a warm person. She already knew what I had done, but she was still nice to me.

When we were alone in her office, I realized that I couldn't look her in the eye. This was something new. I had always been able to keep my head up and talk to anyone face-to-face, but ever since Texas I had had trouble doing that. I could speak when I was looking at the floor, or at a person's shoes, or the wall, anything but their face. I let my eyes wander to the fish tank she kept in the corner and to the windows. As long as I didn't look her in the eye, I could talk.

We covered a lot of territory: the relationship between my parents, how I felt about men, my feelings about marriage, Mark, and the investigation. She asked me about *Frank.* I wasn't willing to call him by that name. The person I had come to love was named Mark. That was the only name I could say.

I told her I didn't want to ever face Mark again, and a trial would force me to do that. I didn't want to be questioned anymore. That is why I was reluctant to go to counseling.

Between my parents and my teammates, I had answered enough questions.

Most of what I said was true, especially the part about not wanting to go through a trial. I shuddered at the idea. But the truth I didn't tell was that I still felt I might one day reestablish a relationship with Mark, perhaps when I was eighteen. I even felt like defending him at times. After all, no one had given me any real reasons why our relationship was wrong. They just said it was bad and demanded I accept that view. I pretended to agree, but only to spare myself the agony of terrible arguments.

I knew that the loyalty I felt for Mark would be hard for anyone to understand. It was difficult for me because, believe it or not, I was also afraid of him. One minute I felt like defending him with my last breath. The next I felt like he was some kind of sicko. I realized this conflict in the middle of a counseling session when the therapist grew very quiet and asked me: "What are you afraid of?"

"There are a lot of windows in my room," I told her. "I'm afraid he might hire someone to shoot me in the middle of the night. Or maybe he'll kidnap me to keep me from testifying."

When she asked me what I wanted to happen in counseling, I told her I thought that would be a better question for my parents because this wasn't my idea. I wanted my life back; I wanted it to be normal again. I didn't say this, but I didn't feel confident about her being able to help me. She seemed too cold, too distant, too concerned about my parents and not concerned enough about me.

Obviously my life was not going to be anything near normal until I got on with counseling, so when David said there would be another interview, with another psychologist, I just agreed to go. The appointment was scheduled for the hour after an evening swim practice. I wondered why my parents hadn't considered that I hated late-night meetings.

Psychologist Number Two met us in the waiting room. This time I wasn't going to go it alone. She invited my mother and David into the room, and we sat on opposite ends of a large sofa.

What would make us sit so far apart? she asked. It seemed like an idiotic question to me, but it got my mother talking. She immediately went into everything that I'd ever done wrong in my life.

I began to cry. "I am not a bad person!" I yelled to try to make her stop.

David came to my aid. "Maybe you are being too hard on her," he said.

I felt like I was back in Texas. I pleaded with my mother to just stop talking. She said she wouldn't because I had caused our family so much anguish. The worst part was that the counselor didn't say a thing. She just sat there as we argued with each other.

When it was over, I knew I didn't want to see this woman ever again. I didn't like her. But I also didn't want to go to another initial interview session. As we drove home, my parents asked me what I thought. It was late at night. I didn't have the energy for a serious discussion. "She was nicer than the first one," I sighed. "I guess she's the one."

Thus therapy began. Week after week I would go to the office, my mind filled with movie images of whacked-out mentally ill people. Was I just like them? I felt too ashamed to talk about the feelings I had for Mark. The psychologist hypothesized that maybe I was looking for a father figure in my life. I didn't know what to say to that.

I did know that I resented someone making up theories about my life. Still, deep down, I hoped that she would become someone that I could learn to trust so that I could talk about all that I was going through. And I looked for any sign that she might understand. I guess I was testing her. When I discussed how my mother lived at the office, and then brought the office home, she suggested that I make appointments with her. Nothing was said about my feelings or how our family's priorities may have been wrong. Schedule appointments, she said.

>>>

It is amazing how a single moment in life can change everything so quickly, including the way people see you. One night, soon after Texas, one of the more active swim team mothers called our house. We had always thought of her as a friend of the family, because her daughter and I had been on the same relay team. We had been friends for more than five years.

"Is your mommy there?" she asked when I answered the phone.

I called my mom and handed her the phone. We were in the kitchen, so it was easy for me to listen in without appearing to be a snoop. I ran the water and had a drink. I poked around in the refrigerator. It wasn't long before the conversation turned into an argument.

"I don't think that's necessary," my mother said.

Pause.

"But nothing happened that could have transmitted anything."

Pause.

"Because she told me."

Pause.

"Yes, I believe her. This is too important. She would not lie about it."

Pause.

"I can understand why you are worried about Katie, but I don't know how any of the other girls could be affected."

Pause.

"Aren't you a nurse? Don't you know how this stuff spreads?"

Pause.

"Well, I'm not going to insist she do any such thing, and I can't believe you called to ask this."

Pause.

"I wouldn't be so quick to say who's the worst parent around. Can you be so sure that the same thing isn't going on under your nose?"

Pause.

"I'm sorry you feel that way."

Pause.

"Well, the feeling is mutual. Good-bye."

By the end, my mother had been yelling into the phone and when she hung up her face was a little flushed. "We're beginning to learn who our friends are," she told me. "That's not such a bad thing, either."

I looked into my mom's eyes. "I'm sorry, Mom, I really am."

"I know, Katie. I am, too."

>>>

Knowing I couldn't stay away forever, I got up the courage to go to school the next day. I was anxious, worried, maybe even paranoid about what people might know. It was not possible that the incident in Texas had stayed a secret. I knew that some of the girls on the team had talked. What I couldn't anticipate was how everyone was taking it.

On the way to my first class I passed a knot of girls—girls I knew—and heard someone say my name. I stopped and tried to listen without being noticed. They said they couldn't believe the stories they had heard about me because I would never do anything like that. I felt comforted, for a moment, hearing that my old reputation would protect me a bit.

The protection of my reputation didn't last long, though. Gradually enough girls confirmed the story, and everyone seemed to believe it. One by one, friends stopped talking to me. If they wanted more proof, all they had to do was look at me. Every other day or so I would break down and cry in the halls or throw up in the bathroom.

During that first week back my guidance counselor met with me many times. I knew she was checking up on me, making sure I wasn't having some sort of breakdown. She tried to help by giving me opportunities in the day to talk. In reality it didn't make things better. She couldn't control what people said behind my back, or the glances that people gave me, or the rumors that ran wild through the school halls. And her vague comments—"I can imagine how bad you feel"—meant nothing to me.

The rumors were ridiculous. Once I was in a bathroom stall when two girls came in and began yapping about me. One girl said she had seen me take a pregnancy test in the school bathroom. Of course, she said it came out positive. A few days later the hot story was that I had used a wire hanger to self-abort the fetus. No one ever confronted me directly with these stories, but I heard them.

It's hard to explain why people would make these things up. On some level, I wondered if they were trying to make my situation—and me—seem as horrible as possible to convince themselves that they were different. If I was just an ordinary girl, someone just like them, then they would have to worry about it happening to them. But if I was a terrible person, terrible beyond belief, then they could be sure they were safe.

And as much as they needed to make me into someone awful, I needed a way to understand them, so I could at least keep going to school. I decided to believe that they had just forgotten to consider how I might feel. If they knew the pain I was in, they would stop talking, stop making it worse.

No matter what their reasons or motivations, the gossip hurt. Very few of my old friends wanted to associate with me, and even those who may have wanted to felt they couldn't. Their parents wouldn't allow it. To them I wasn't the victim of a crime who deserved compassion. I had been stupid, or maybe seductive, and placed myself in danger. I was a bad influence.

I tried to act normally, to be brave, and I hoped that people would start treating me again like the old Katie Tarbox. At times I was fine, but then the feelings of isolation and rejection would come back, hard. I spent a lot of time thinking about how bad I was. I would compare myself to other kids. I would think about how my teachers knew what had happened. I always reached the same conclusion. I was the worst person, the worst student, in the place.

One day, in Latin class, I got lost in these kinds of thoughts and just started crying. I raised my hand and was allowed to leave. Karen followed me and, for a moment, I thought something good and normal from my life before—my friendship with Karen—might be coming back.

"Here," she said, ripping some toilet paper off a roll and handing it to me. I took it and wiped the tears off my face.

"This isn't going to last forever, you know," she said.

"It feels like it will," I said.

"You've got to pull yourself together, Katie. If you don't, it's not going to stop. You have to show them it doesn't bother you."

It felt good to have Karen take my side. But this didn't mean the renewal of our relationship. She looked at me once more, to make sure the tears had stopped, and then turned and walked out. It would be the very last moment of our friendship.

As much as I tried to take Karen's advice, Texas, Mark, and the long-term deception I had practiced came back again and again to slap me in the face. One Saturday, while I was at an all-day rehearsal for an all-state chorus concert, my mom went to her office to clear up some work and pay some bills. She opened the phone bill and found the phone calls that I had placed to Mark.

Life brings humor, or maybe it was irony, even at the darkest moments, which may explain why my mom mistakenly dialed a psychiatric hospital when she was trying to verify that the calls were indeed to his house. She hung up, dialed again—more carefully—and waited with her heart pounding. When Mark answered, for some reason all she thought to say was "Connecticut Telephone Company."

Something about the phone bill, knowing that I had been making all those calls and she never realized it, made my mother think that we needed more than a housekeeper in our home, at least for a while. She wanted someone else, someone in the family, around at all times, just in case Mark tried to contact me. My grandparents—all four of them—agreed to come and stay at our house.

This would be a big change for me, since I had spent so much time alone. I was being treated like a baby and it was humiliating. It would go on at least until summer. It felt like a punishment, not only for me, but for my grandparents, who had to pick up and move out of their houses. I was embarrassed that they knew about all of this, and angry because every relationship I had was being damaged.

When I told my mother about my feelings, she surprised me with her response. She said I *should* feel bad that my grandparents had to come to our house. I had to take the blame. This hurt. Even though they didn't punish me, my parents were obviously blaming me. I knew that what had happened was at least in part my fault, but I hated hearing it.

I would hear it more than once. In fact, blaming would become a regular part of our conversations about what had happened. We would also talk about my mom's struggle to understand how angry she was at me. She would tell me it is possible to love someone and hate them simultaneously. She hoped our relationship would not turn that way, but she felt it was going down that path.

>>>

My mother's phone call to Mark's house on that Saturday morning may have ignited a flame. On Monday Mark telephoned our house. Abby answered and at first he thought it was me. When he realized it wasn't me, he asked to speak with my mother. Abby told him that my mother wasn't home, and when she asked who was calling he said "a close friend" and then hung up.

This first call began a stream of calls that made me feel embarrassed, annoyed, and even lonely for him. Over and over again we would hang up on him. Finally, Mark left a message on our machine expressing his desire to make a donation to our "favorite charity." It was obvious he knew he was in serious trouble and hoped that we could be bought. We never answered him, but we did tell the police about all of his calls.

The police were becoming a big part of my life. The detectives in Texas asked the New Canaan police to do a more formal and detailed interview with me, and of course we agreed. At around 8:30 one school night, after I was finished swimming, my grandmother walked me into the police station. I was introduced to the sergeant who was going to conduct the interview and to a woman officer who was there for my comfort. I said good-bye to my grandmother and was led into an office.

The officers reassured me meeting wouldn't take long or be difficult. I only wish they had been right. Before we even got started with the questions we ran into trouble. Neither of the officers was at all familiar with the Internet. It took half an hour for me to explain it to them.

When we finally got to the questions, I had a lot of trouble understanding their relevance to the investigation. They kept asking me: "Are your parents mad at you because of the incident?"

"I don't think mad describes it correctly," I told them. "Of course they were angry with Mark but not me. Their feelings toward me could be better described as disappointment. I was their daughter who had always been so responsible. Now I had violated their trust. They were not mad. They were heartbroken."

Mostly the police wanted to understand the exact sequence of the events that night. I hated talking about it. It was late in the day. I was tired to begin with, but this process made me feel exhausted, and I just wanted to get it over with as soon as possible. But the questioning went on for hours. It was a strange scene. Me answering all these questions. The officers trying to figure out how to respond to me. They gave me jelly beans and a fake police badge and chatted to make the time go by quicker, but time really doesn't go fast in a police station. When the questions stopped, my grandmother and I had to wait for them to type up the interview so that we could verify the report.

At about 10:45, the report was done and we read it. I signed it, verifying that it was the truth to the best of my knowledge. Later my mother signed it as my legal guardian. This was yet another strange thing, to my mind. She wasn't there during any of the interview. She wasn't involved in my relationship with Mark, and she wasn't there in that hotel room. How could she guarantee that I had told the truth to the best of my knowledge?

Everything fades with time. A few weeks passed and even though I was still filled with regret and confusion, I began to accept that everyone thought they knew what had happened to me in Texas. I even began to accept that I could not do much of anything about their opinions of me.

Through all of this, I tried to continue with the life of a kid, pretending that I was somehow in a normal situation. That spring my singing group went on a tour of Washington, D.C. It was the seventy-fifth anniversary of the Lincoln Memorial, and musical groups from every state were invited to come and perform on the monument's steps. In addition to that performance, we also sang at a veteran's hospital and outside the White House. I went as part of the group, and I have no doubt that a lot of people wondered if I was going to meet up with Mark somewhere along the way.

I hoped that my mother would be able to attend these performances, considering it would be one of the last times I would sing with the choir. But as always, business was a conflict, and she was not able to make it. So I was alone, in more ways than one, among twenty kids, all dressed in red sweaters, black shorts, and black tights. Everyone stood in rows according to height, and we must have seemed like generic kids—carefree, happy.

I felt very removed from all of the other kids at the event. I wasn't anything like the girl next to me, even though I had my hair done the same way and wore the same clothes. I had broken off with Mark, but he was still dominating my thoughts.

I missed Mark. And if this crisis had been about anything else, I would have turned to him for support, as I had in the past. I missed hearing his voice late at night. I missed the notes on the Internet. He would have made me laugh. He would be the one making me feel loved. And I was convinced that since I still thought about him in the same way he must also be feeling the same. It didn't matter much that he had openly lied about his age or name, I just wanted Mark back. I wanted to feel again the way he had made me feel when we were close.

Ashley was the only one who didn't abandon me completely. She was there the day when Karen approached me at lunchtime. Karen didn't look happy, and I knew there was something wrong when she asked to speak with me outside the lunchroom. Like the time she had told me about her brother's leukemia, she suggested that we go to the bathroom. It was the only private place left for two girls who had once shared so much during sleep-overs and long late-night phone calls.

Karen didn't waste any time. "I have to be honest with you, Katie," she said. "I don't consider you a close friend anymore." I knew it was true. I had lost my old best friend months ago. But just as it was painful for me to hear my mother blame me for things, it was painful to hear Karen tell the truth about us.

I asked her why she felt this way, because I needed an explanation. She told me that I hadn't been there for her for months, or for her brother's illness. She was right. I hadn't offered her much support at all, but she had also pulled away from me, and she had asked me not to talk to her about Rob. She said she felt bad about telling me this now, but she had to do this for herself. She needed to clear the air. She was dealing with a life-and-death situation in her family.

I couldn't argue with her, and I didn't want to. But it was hard to let go of the idea, the hope, that Karen and I could be friends again. I was confused and frustrated. I was so upset that I went to the school nurse and said I was sick and had to leave school.

My grandmother picked me up that day. I didn't know what to say to her, and she didn't know what to say to me to make me feel better.

As soon I got home I called my mom at work. She didn't have to tell me that I had let Karen down. I knew that. What I didn't know was that Karen's brother was really in danger. His wasn't ordinary leukemia, my mom said, it was a more serious type, and his chances for survival were not good at all. This came as a complete surprise. In the fall I had been told that Rob was doing well, and because the doctors had caught the leukemia early he was going to survive. No one even mentioned that this disease could be terminal, and I thought that because he was in remission he would be okay.

Back in the bathroom at school, Karen had berated me for not asking her about her brother's condition. I should have done more to cheer her up, she said, brought her cupcakes and balloons every so often. But I couldn't have understood her suffering because she had never told me the truth.

At the time, I blamed all of this on her, and my feelings of outrage about the situation were a distraction from my own personal crisis. I felt that it was extremely selfish for Karen to dump this on me now. And as horrible as it may seem, I also thought my problem was worse than hers. It would take me a long time to accept that Karen was right and to realize that I should have been a better friend.

After I finished talking to my mom, I went up to my room and began eating Godiva chocolate Easter eggs. I think I ate ten of them while I tried several times to call Karen. Her mom told me Karen wasn't home, even though I could hear her in the background. Eventually I got her on the phone. I told her I wanted to be friends. I understood her feelings, but we had been so close, it seemed we should be able to be friends again. Karen said no, we were through as friends.

I took some solace in my friendship with Ashley, but this relationship was under pressure, too, from her parents. One Saturday they called and asked if they might come over to speak with my mother and David. They all sat downstairs in the family room, and as I walked by, on my way out to swimming practice, I could feel the tension.

Like other swim team parents, they didn't feel comfortable having me around their daughter, even though Ashley and I had been close for a long time. They told my parents that I wasn't a good influence on her, but because we were so close and I was Ashley's friend they would let Ashley decide how she wanted to handle it. For now, she would be my friend. That was her decision, but her parents were not happy with me at all.

I didn't understand why they couldn't accept that people make mistakes, especially teenagers. Didn't they understand that I wasn't entirely responsible for what happened? Mark had played a huge role, but everyone ignored that fact. I thought that we all deserved second chances in life. But I had made such a big mistake, done something so shameful, that no one seemed able to forgive me.

I lost more friends on the swim team as all the parents began to agree that I was a dangerous influence. My sister Carrie, who was on my swim team, too, was also ostracized, and so were my parents. And through it all, Mark was free out in California. Now, when I thought of him, I sometimes pictured him talking to another girl over the Internet and trying to get her into bed.

Victim

>>>

With summer, I got a break from school, but not from New Canaan. Before it had always seemed like no one even noticed me, but now it seemed like everyone in town was either gossiping about me, looking at me strangely, or judging me silently. Of course, I'll never know how much of this was really happening and how much I was imagining because of my shame. But I heard enough to be sure I was widely known as either The Girl Who Got Molested or New Canaan's Lolita.

Everyone was a little too interested in my sexual attitudes and behavior. I guess this is something every girl learns to deal with, eventually. Adults are intrigued and frightened by young female bodies. We're supposed to be attractive. The media make us into some kind of powerful ideal. But this power is also evil. We're bad if we think about sex or act sexual. Good girls never ever do that.

My parents could see how much I was suffering. This didn't mean we actually talked about it. Counseling—which my family made sure to tell me was a pretty narcissistic exercise—was supposed to take care of my need for talking. Outside of the psychologist's office I was to make the best of things, get on with life.

Still, my mother and David wanted to help, so they decided I should spend four weeks at a summer camp in the Florida Keys. It was going to be the first trip that I took by myself since the Texas incident. It showed me that they had begun to trust me again. They drove me to JFK early on a Sunday morning to say good-bye to me. I hugged them and promised to call as soon as I arrived in Miami.

At camp I became a certified scuba diver and was able to go diving at Looe Key, one of the very few coral reefs in U.S. territory, almost every day. Being around people my age who didn't know what had happened to me was therapeutic. For those four weeks I felt like myself again, and I went home feeling relaxed and maybe even happy.

When I got home from Florida my parents seemed to be more themselves, too. But we all knew that the investigation was continuing, and, in fact, things were not settled. David insisted I still had to continue counseling with Psychologist Number Two. I was very immature, in his eyes, and I had some big lessons to learn.

I couldn't have disagreed more. Hadn't Mark, my family, Karen, even the whole town of New Canaan been teaching me harsh lessons for a long time now?

I never did understand therapy, but I went because my mother and David insisted. And so, in addition to being a slut and a victim, I became a mental patient. The psychologist offered absolutely no direction to any of our conversations. I would talk for about twenty minutes straight and then she would say, "Yes, and how do you *feel* about that?"

Since I was forced into treatment, I resented the whole idea. I wasn't sent to therapy for me. Well, in part my mother was worried about me, but she was mainly trying to please all the other swim team parents. This is how it went: If Katie's in therapy, then she's obviously getting help and therefore the Tarbox family can stay in the swimming group.

I complained about the counseling every day. My mother listened, in part because she felt the same way about the therapist. We were both having a difficult time relating to Psychologist Number Two. Eventually she and David had a dispute about whether I had to continue counseling. Since my mother wears the pants, I didn't have to continue.

I did have to continue with the whole legal process, however. None of us had a choice about that. And the case was about to take a serious turn. Because Mark had used the Internet to find me, and I had crossed state lines to meet him, the case was covered by federal laws. The FBI was taking over the investigation, and I would have to go to their office in New Haven for yet another interview and a polygraph test, which Mark's lawyers had demanded in exchange for his agreeing to take one, too.

For some reason, the New Canaan police were going to be involved in transferring the case to the FBI. On the day of the polygraph test, David and I drove to the police station early in the morning. It was just the two of us, because my mom was in Minnesota on a business trip. We spoke the night before, and she emphasized that I must tell the truth, the whole truth.

The New Canaan sergeant who had been investigating the case planned to drive us to the FBI office in New Haven, where the polygraph test would be given. I was afraid—I didn't want to be hooked up to machines that would determine whether or not I was telling the truth. Even though I knew I was telling the truth, at times I doubted myself. I think I expected the machine to tell me whether I was telling the truth, even though I knew I was.

The police car we rode in was equipped with a barrier that turned the backseat into a rolling jail cell for arrested suspects and protected the officers riding in front. I, of course, had to be the one who sat back there while David rode in the front.

When we pulled up to the federal building in New Haven, I immediately spotted the FBI shield. Inside, photographs of the president and vice president were hung over the doors to the elevator. I was feeling more and more intimidated and afraid. When the elevator finally came, the three of us rode silently up to the floor where the interview would be conducted.

When we arrived, Special Agent Ronald Barndollar, who would be handling the case, was waiting for us. He shook my hand and then immediately focused on David. "Can you wait outside for a few minutes?" he asked me. I stepped into the hallway, feeling cold and a little small. Men and women scurried by—I guessed they were lawyers or FBI agents—and each one glanced at me, probably wondering what a teenager was doing there.

When David and Agent Barndollar returned, they said nothing about what they had discussed. "We're going to do this in a special room," said the agent, and he led us to a tiny, windowless little space that was completely bare except for a polygraph machine, a table, and three chairs. A two-way mirror filled one wall.

Two agents and I crowded into this small place. "That's a two-way mirror and there are people on the other side," said Agent Barndollar. "Assistant United States Attorney Gates Garrity-Rokous, who will handle your case, and some other people. First we'll do a regular interview, and they're going to listen. Later we'll do the polygraph. Okay?"

In our conversation Agent Barndollar seemed to labor

over the smallest points. We had to first establish what I called this man they knew as Francis John Kufrovich. I told him that I called him Mark, because that was the person I met on the Internet and came to know as a close friend. Frank was a different person, a stranger everyone was determined to put in jail. I didn't know him, and so I continued to talk about Mark.

They took out several copies of an affidavit Mark had signed and placed them on the table. I began laughing when I saw the word *affidavit* was misspelled in the middle of the page, dark and bold. I read it to myself as one of them read aloud. Mark admitted to meeting me on-line. He failed to mention that he had asked me if I was a virgin during one of our talks. And he falsely claimed that we kept our relationship secret to protect my mother because "at age 15 she had had a very bad sexual experience with an older man."

Many of the things Mark said made me begin to lose sympathy for him and start to see why everyone else wanted him locked up. He said that I had pressed to see him in person, which was the absolute opposite of the truth. He said I proposed different "circumstances where we could meet." And it was only after he had mentioned he was going to Dallas for business that I informed him of my swim meet there. In short, I was a stalker. In Dallas, "the presence of Katie standing in a robe at my door concerned me quite a bit," he wrote. Throughout his statement he claimed he told me that I should have made my parents aware of this relationship.

When we finished going over Mark's version of things, the agents asked me why I had ever trusted him. They wondered why I didn't recognize him as a creep. I told them that I had thought I was getting involved with a much younger and respectable person. My parents weren't really home a lot and I just looked to Mark as someone to talk with. I couldn't see anything wrong with that.

We then went through some e-mails. They would read them and ask me to interpret them, or explain to them how they made me feel. It didn't take a rocket scientist to figure it out. Mark's e-mails often said things like, "Katie I think you are the most wonderful person in the world." Even though I tried not to show that even now I had feelings for Mark, I think they could tell.

The most difficult thing for me was explaining in vivid detail the physical contact that night in the hotel, and the series of events that followed. They wanted to get it exactly right so they asked many follow-up questions. I explained how I was wearing three shirts that night, and it wasn't as if I was making it easy for him to grab me. He had to put some effort into it. I apologized for not being able to look them in the eye while I spoke. I told them it was a problem that I had, and it wasn't them.

When we were finished with all the questions, the agents said we could take a break before the lie-detector test. We walked down the hall to a little kitchen where I got a Diet Coke.

When I walked back into the room, the chair I had been sitting in was turned to face the wall. I had told everyone I was willing to cooperate, and I was still willing, but I had to fight the impulse to flee. No matter what anyone said, I felt like I was on trial. Now I was going to be strapped to this machine, like a murderer condemned to the electric chair. I looked at the setup and decided to just stand there until I was told to do otherwise.

"Just relax, Katie," said one of the agents. "This doesn't hurt at all, and after a little while you'll even forget the machine."

"Okay."

"I'm going to ask you a series of questions, in different order, several times. These questions have simple yes or no answers. Some of them will be ordinary things, just questions about you. The rest will be about this case. Your blood pressure, pulse, and rate of breathing will all be monitored as you respond."

I just stood there, frozen. He told me to sit down, so we could get started.

I sat down in the chair and the agent went to work. He clamped a sensor to the tip of my right index finger. A cord went across my rib cage to measure breathing, and a blood pressure cuff was wrapped around my arm. It was hard to believe that these machines were going to record and calculate whether I was telling the truth.

"Is your name Katherine Tarbox?"

"Yes."

"Do you like to sing?"

"Yes."

"Did Mark touch your breasts?"

"Yes."

"Did Mark attempt to touch your crotch area?"

"Yes."

"Other than the times we talked about, have you ever told a lie?"

"No."

"Did you know Mark before?"

"Yes."

The same questions were asked over and over again, but in a different order. I tried to stay calm, and eventually I did relax a little. When it was over, I asked the question that everyone probably asks at the end of a polygraph: "Was I lying?"

"You tell me," said the agent.

"No, I wasn't."

The agent got up, unhooked all the equipment, and then told me he would be right back. He left the room for about five seconds and returned with David. They stood and I sat as the polygrapher announced that I had been very consistent in my answers, except for one question, the one about lying.

I knew why. I was telling the truth, but thinking about the lies I had told had made me worry and that had made all the indexes—blood pressure, pulse, breathing—rise. That, they told me, was normal. Apparently everyone gets tense with that question.

When I was finally free to go, I went to a phone and called my mother, who was in Minneapolis on business. "Good news," I said. "They say I'm not lying." I was glad that it was on the record. I couldn't wait to hear the results from Mark's tests. I was certain they wouldn't provide similar outcomes.

While I was on the phone, I could overhear David asking the FBI agents a million questions about my case, how the polygraph worked, even how they investigated crimes. Even after I got off the phone, he just kept on talking, and I could tell by their faces they were exasperated.

"When will Mark be charged?" asked David. "When will this go to trial? What chance do we have for a conviction?"

It seemed to me that he was enjoying it, and as we left, one of the agents told him he had watched too many cop shows on TV. I smiled to myself and thought, That's probably true.

>>>

For a long time, all I wanted was for my life to be what it was before that night in Texas. But that was asking for the impossible. My life would never be the same. For one thing, I was through with swimming.

I had felt like quitting before, but this time I wasn't going to change my mind. I just hated the water. I never wanted to go to practice. It wasn't that it reminded me of the Texas incident. It was more that I just hated swimming because the people on the team and their parents had been so mean to me. I thought they were my friends, but they had turned against me and it wasn't hard, then, for me to let go of the team.

Other things began to change, too. The most significant was Ashley's decision to go to boarding school in England the next year rather than to New Canaan High. I couldn't believe what I was hearing. Not only was I losing my best friend, I was losing my *only* friend. I would begin high school with its usual challenges without the comfort of even one kind face.

I said good-bye to Ashley on a Wednesday night in August. She and her mother picked me up at my house in their hunter green Land Rover. When I got in I was already thinking about saying good-bye. Still, all during the drive to the Japanese restaurant where we would have dinner, I tried to act as if nothing unusual was happening.

"You all packed?" I asked.

"I only have to buy a dressing gown in England," she said.

"A what?" I asked, smiling.

"I guess you Yanks would call it a bathrobe," she answered.

I walked into the restaurant feeling close to Ashley, deeply grateful for her loyal friendship. I couldn't help but think about that little hillside in Texas where we rolled over and over until we reached the bottom, laughing.

Ashley and I sat down at the sushi bar and ordered. The night passed so quickly that soon we had consumed our green tea ice cream and it was time to leave. Since Ashley's mom had dropped us off, my mom took us home, and when we pulled into Ashley's driveway I told her, "I'll see you soon," knowing that I wouldn't.

I didn't cry. I knew she had to go, just as my older sister Abby would soon leave for private school in New Hampshire. The next morning, as Abby was leaving, I heard her shoes on the hardwood floor in my room. It was about six o'clock. I opened my eyes and got out of bed, feeling the legs of my pajama pants fall to the ground, covering my feet.

"Bye, Katie," said Abby, as if it was no big deal.

"I love you, Abby." I leaned over to hug her and pulled on her golden curly hair to see how long it was, just like I always did.

"I love you, too."

And then she was gone. I pulled the drapes closed over the window, got back into bed, and started to cry. Everyone was leaving me. Soon I would be back at school, more alone than ever before. It was not going to be a good year.

>>>

I began high school a couple of days later. Most kids would be excited about this milestone, but I dreaded it. I got up on time, rode to school with David, and forced myself to put one foot ahead of the other so I could get through the door and down the hallway.

All that day I kept waiting for someone to say something to me about Texas, but it didn't happen. So much had happened in everyone's life that summer that my little scandal was ancient history. This didn't mean I was suddenly popular. Most people still kept their distance, even as I passed them between classes. But most of the gossiping was over.

I enrolled in all honors classes and two languages, so I

was very busy. It was an academic grind with little relief. I did homework for hours every night and spent my weekends alone. This was nothing like what I imagined high school would be from watching *90210*. I didn't go to parties. I didn't hang out with friends and laugh all night long. I was lonesome and, worse, bored.

Up in New Hampshire Abby reported that she was anything but bored. It was not long before I started to think that boarding school would be a good idea for me, too. My parents thought it would offer me a new start, which I needed. We made a list of seven schools that I would look at, and then I applied to five.

It was a bit like applying for college. I had to fill out applications, take aptitude tests, write essays, and go for interviews, which meant for seven weekends in a row I spent my Saturdays at these schools. We would wake up early, drive to a Dunkin' Donuts, and visit a school before driving home. Eventually we narrowed the choices to three, all of them in New Hampshire: Phillips Exeter Academy, St. Paul's School, and Deerfield Academy. Deerfield was supposed to be the least difficult to get into, and it was also my favorite. It had a wonderful swimming pool, and an atmosphere that felt a little less pressured. I imagined that I could be very happy there.

The trips to these schools gave my mother and me hours for talking, and we used them. Gradually my mother said she was no longer angry with me and we were getting over the Texas incident. We didn't really talk about the whole legal process that was still moving forward, or the fact that there might one day be a trial. My main concern was piecing my life back together and preparing to go away next year. But as time passed, I always had the case in the back of my mind, and I kept expecting the phone to ring with some news from the FBI or the federal prosecutor in New Haven.

I dreaded hearing from the FBI because I knew that when they called I would be forced back into the role of victim-or-slut and that Mark would be one step closer to being arrested. And as often as other people said how much they wished to see Mark locked up, I still couldn't agree. I did not believe that he was a criminal. His behavior had been inappropriate, at least in Texas. But I couldn't understand why it was illegal for someone—even a forty-one-year-old man—to travel to Texas to meet me.

When you think about what had happened in that hotel room, it was not as big a deal as everything that happened afterward. The way everyone—my family, the swim team, school friends, teachers—had reacted had made it much worse. And while they were all saying that they were upset about what had happened to me, no one seemed very interested in accepting me or comforting me. Instead, they talked about how I was responsible, how I had let everyone down, disgraced myself, behaved terribly. It almost seemed like they were saying I got what I deserved.

Escape

>>>

This may be hard for you to believe, but it's true. Although we hadn't spoken in more than a year, I still felt close to Mark, or close to the idea of him. I still cared for him and worried about his future. I also believed that he cared about me. No one knew I had these feelings, not even Psychologist Number Two. I kept them secret from her and my parents because I knew they wouldn't understand, especially in light of the information we were getting about him.

Every few weeks or so, the FBI or the prosecutor would call to fill us in. We learned that Mark had pursued other girls—and boys—and he had slept with some of them. A search of his house turned up pornography downloaded from the Internet, including a picture of a young girl involved in intercourse.

Eventually every girl has to come to grips with the existence of pornography. But when I first realized there was such a thing I found it disgusting. I thought the women who were involved were pathetic, and that it was degrading to everyone. It was hard to understand why adults were involved in it, and the more I understood how widespread it was, the more gross it seemed. At first I thought only a very few people were involved with pornography. When you realize that millions and millions of people are into pornography, you have to figure some of them are people you know, and the world isn't really what you think it is at all.

It's probably seminormal for a bunch of college kids in a frat house to want to watch X-rated movies. It's not just guys, of course. I know at least one girl who's pretty obsessed with her collection of porn videos. Guys are just so hormonal, though, that I think it's better for them to have pornography than to go out and take advantage of someone. I thought it was like a safety valve or something. But if you're over twenty-five, or married, and you really need it, there's something wrong. And if you really need pictures of little kids, then you are definitely sick.

>>>

I managed to forget Mark until one day late in July, when I answered a call from an FBI agent who asked me if my parents were home. I got my mom and listened. From my mother's part of the conversation I could tell that Mark's arraignment would be the next day. No one had bothered to tell me this was coming up, which made me a bit angry, but I was getting used to hearing myself discussed and watching other people control what would happen to me. Sometimes I resented it, but at other times I was glad to be left out. When my mother got off the phone, she and David told me they were both going, but that I would stay home.

Eventually I would sit down with a tape recording of the arraignment, snap it into a Walkman, and listen hard to every word. It began with the prosecutor. He revealed that Mark had used alcohol and pornography to entice other victims. He had taken trips with minors to different parts of the country, buying their tickets with their first name and his last name. He was also in a relationship with a twenty-year-old woman, whose virginity he had taken when she was just fourteen. Her name was Miss Jennifer Jones, she was a student at the University of California–Davis, and she kept a journal of every time they had sex together.

The judge then asked Mark a few basic questions about his life in California and his business. His answers were not revealing, but the way he spoke was. He was so quiet that I had to struggle to hear him. He mumbled his way along until the moment came for him to plead guilty or not guilty. Then he literally shouted, "Not guilty!"

He was so loud that my ears hurt. It was as if he truly believed he was innocent, that I had been in the wrong. I was shaken by the sudden power in his voice and suddenly swept with anxiety. As much as the trial was going to be about Mark's guilt or innocence, it was also going to be about mine. This was going to be a battle over the truth that would define me as either a victim or a lying slut.

The court appearance made the case a public matter, and since this was the first time the federal government had prosecuted an Internet pedophile, it was big news. When I got home from work I turned on the television. As the newscasters spoke about a "minor" who went to Texas and was molested, I found it hard to associate that girl with me. I mean, I knew it was me, but that day in the hotel was so far in the past.

On the morning after the arraignment, the newspaper headlines announced MAN CALLED INTERNET SEDUCER and CALIFORNIA MAN PLEADS INNOCENT TO SEX CHARGES. The articles forced me to look at Mark in a different light. He was described as an accused criminal, a suspected pedophile, the target of a very serious prosecution. Having it laid out in black and white—and so publicly—gave the accusations a weight they didn't have until now with me. The reporters were outside observers. They didn't know me; they didn't know Mark. Unlike the FBI and the prosecutors, whose jobs were focused on convicting people, they had no interest in either side. But they were describing me as a victim and him as an accused perpetrator. For a moment I thought, If they believe it, maybe I should, too.

Gradually, the man who had been my friend, who had listened to me and cared for me so deeply, was fading from view. He was being replaced by the image of a manipulative, porn-obsessed, child molester named Frank Kufrovich. This was not my Mark. But he was the one who had created Mark. I wondered if Mark represented the good man that this Frank had hoped he could be. Mark was the positive one, but he wasn't strong enough to overcome Frank's sickness. Instead, he always ended up serving Frank. I still liked Mark, but it seemed as if he only existed in my heart, and he was dying. Frank was the reality, and I now began to call him by that name.

That fall I left for private school. We decided on St. Paul's in New Hampshire, where Abby had gone. She was proud that I had chosen her school, and I was glad to be going someplace where my name might not be known. I thought it would be easy to leave home, but I began to feel lonesome even while I was loading the car in our driveway. I needed to leave, almost felt forced to do it. But I was still just fifteen years old, and I started to miss my family during the drive to New Hampshire.

The sight of the campus—worn brick classroom buildings, white clapboard houses—made me feel better. Abby had been happy at St. Paul's, so I thought that I could be happy there, too. And the people were open and kind. But as friendly as they were, I still wondered: If they knew what I had done—what had been done to me—would they be so nice? I decided that I'd rather not find out. I could control what people at St. Paul's knew about me. And I would keep Frank, Texas, and all the rest of it secret.

Unlike New Canaan High School, where it seemed only the more advanced students studied hard, everyone at St. Paul's was serious about academics. They not only kept us busy with schoolwork but also expected us to participate in extracurricular activities. I played on the field hockey team, sang in the chorus, and continued with piano. I was also able to make new friends. I was closest to my roommate, a girl named Penn, who came from a wealthy North Carolina family. She was not, by any definition, a Southern belle. In fact, when we first met, I thought she must be from New York City. She wore funky Armani glasses, brown tortoiseshell with squarish frames. Like me, Penn had come to St. Paul's to build her own identity, outside of her hometown and family.

For the first time since I began my relationship with Frank I felt like a normal teenager. Slowly I began to regain my confidence. As colder nights began to turn the leaves red, yellow, and bright orange, I began to think that no one at St. Paul's was ever going to find out about my past. The case against Frank would no doubt appear in the news again, but because I was a minor, my name would never be mentioned. So even if someone at St. Paul's happened to read about the case, how would they associate it with me? It wasn't going to happen, and this thought made me feel better than I had felt in a long time.

Guilty

>>>

The defendant—the man who had opened the door wearing those god-awful white shoes, groped me on the sofa, and been arrested by the police in Dallas—was Frank. I still remembered Mark—sweet, caring, intelligent, funny, and I still missed him. But this man Frank was determined to make me miserable, to create months, even years of conflict just so he wouldn't have to admit or take responsibility for what he had done. During the week before Thanksgiving in 1997 he sent out his private detectives to question my teachers, my neighbors, and my biological father. They pestered Karen with questions about me when her brother was literally days from death. Was my mother neglectful? Had I been beaten? I wasn't worried that they might find something scandalous about me or my family. I wasn't a Lolita. And the worst thing they could find out was that we don't go to church on Sundays and sometimes we mix our recycling in with our trash.

But I knew they would soon show up at St. Paul's. My refuge was going to be invaded, and much of the power I had gained in going away—power over who knew what about me—was lost. Night after night I lay awake, filled with worry, and when I finally did fall asleep, it wouldn't last. I'd wake up at two, or three, or four with my heart pounding and my mind racing. On those nights I'd take a book, a pillow, and a blanket into the bathroom and settle on the floor under the sink and wait for dawn.

During the day, every time I walked into my room I feared that I would find a private detective sitting there. I began to feel like I was falling apart. I had to tell someone about my anxiety. My mother had called the rector of the school and explained that I had something serious to discuss. I met with him shortly after. I know he was surprised by what I told him, because I had seemed like such a happy student. But he didn't judge me negatively; rather, he seemed to care about my safety. He said that the campus was private. Anyone who came without permission would be asked to leave.

The only other person I felt I had to tell was Penn. She was my roommate, and if they were going to bother anyone it would be her. So one afternoon when we were alone in our room I decided to tell her. I sat on my bed and cleared my throat. She looked up from the desk where she was studying and put down her pen.

"I've got something serious to talk to you about," I began.

"Katie, what are you so nervous about?"

"It's really serious, Penn. After you hear this you might decide you don't want to be my friend. Other people have done that."

"Katie, you're scaring me. What is it?"

"All right. But you have to let me tell you the whole thing, without interrupting me. Promise?"

"Promise."

"Well, you know America Online, and the whole chat room thing? Two years ago I met this guy on there. His name was Mark. He was extremely nice, Penn, like nobody I had ever met. Anyway, we talked back and forth for six months."

"So?"

"Well, he said he was twenty-three. And I agreed to meet him in Texas at a swim meet. It was a big secret. I didn't tell anybody. But when I got to his room he was a lot older than twenty-three, and he started grabbing me. Then my mother came pounding on the door, and the police came, and everybody found out. They're pressing charges and it's become a really big deal. Nobody here knows about it, except you."

I searched her face for a reaction. She didn't seem shocked or disappointed in me. Instead, she seemed worried. "It's terrible what happened to you," she said. "Are you all right now?"

"I'm okay," I told her, which was almost true. "But the thing is, there's going to be a trial and he might send some investigators up here to try to dig up dirt about me and my family. They could come to see you. I'm sorry."

"Don't be. If they come, I won't talk to them, and I won't let them bother me."

>>>

We braced ourselves for the worst from Frank. I imagined he would send a team of trench-coat-wearing detectives after us, that they would dig through our trash and interrogate our friends and dorm mates. But nothing like this happened. Finally, at Christmastime, my mother called with some news. "What would you think," she asked, "about Frank pleading guilty?"

She explained that Frank's attorneys were in New Haven and that the government had presented them a plea agreement. Frank would serve twelve to twenty-one months in prison in exchange for admitting to a variety of federal charges. It was not much time, considering that the charges he faced carried sentences of up to twenty years. But the prosecutors were not absolutely certain they would get a conviction, partly because the laws were so new. and partly because Frank had been able to pass one of his polygraph tests (although two more said he was lying). If Frank took their offer, at least he would be punished in some way.

My parents hoped he would take the offer because they wanted to spare me the trauma of having to testify in front of a jury. "I don't want you to have to sit through a trial and relive it over and over," said my mother.

I didn't care about that, but I also didn't want to see this drag on and on. I knew that if we won the first time around, there would surely be an appeal. This thing could dominate my life for years. If Frank pleaded guilty it would mean that he would have to admit to the crimes. It meant that my version of the truth would be upheld. That was more important to me than anything. Maybe then I would be able to resume some kind of normal life.

Frank signed the plea agreement on his forty-third birthday, December 29, 1997. I wondered what it felt like for him to finally take responsibility for what had happened in that hotel room in Texas. But I wasn't especially happy that day. The court couldn't change what had happened to me and restore all my destroyed relationships. It was the dead of winter and I saw nothing but mountains of dirty snow on the ground everywhere in New Hampshire. It was getting dark early every day and I still just wanted to sleep.

Maybe I would feel differently when he entered his plea in person, at the courthouse, and I would be there to watch him. Dates for this event were set and changed three or four times. As I waited, I celebrated my sixteenth birthday at school with pizza and a cake.

I couldn't understand why people make a big deal about turning sixteen. If you accept what the media says, and what half the adult world seems to think, adolescence is supposed to be the sweetest slice of life. Maybe it is for some people, but Frank had made sure it wasn't for me. I could only hope that the future would bring less confusion, less pain, less heartache.

Frank's guilty plea was set for March 13, 1998, during my spring break from school. That morning I woke up and went running. Frost covered the ground and clouds blocked the light from the rising sun. I ran and ran and ran, and as I turned for home I thought about what was ahead of me that day. I understood that Frank was ready to admit that he had committed crimes, as defined by the law. But that didn't feel like enough. I wanted him to feel real guilt, real remorse, real responsibility. But as I ran for home, I wondered whether Frank had the capacity to feel empathy for another human being. He would never feel bad about what he had done to me and other people my age.

I had thought that all along I would be perfectly happy with him just pleading guilty. But now that the time was here, I realized that I wanted more, something that was practically impossible. I began to pick up speed, running faster. I wanted Frank to understand the magnitude of his actions, that his crimes were truly wrong not just because of the law.

Out of breath, I reached my house and went inside to shower and change. I tried out my whole wardrobe that morning—suits, dresses, pants, skirts—you name it, I had it on. Nothing pleased me and I became disgusted with everything in my closet. I couldn't understand why I had bought half the things that filled it. Finally I decided on a simple black skirt, white shirt, and black blazer. I brushed my hair and headed out to the car with David.

As we pulled out of the driveway, I was a little disappointed that my mother wasn't there with me. She was in Florida on business. I knew she wanted to be there, but she was giving a major presentation, which she couldn't reschedule. While I admire how hard she works for our family, I thought this was an important day, and I wish she could have been there.

I didn't say much in the car. I stayed busy, tuning the radio. For once David didn't complain about it. We both knew that this would be the first time since Texas that I would see Frank. I don't know if my brain was playing tricks on me, or if I had genuinely forgotten what he looked like, but I couldn't remember his face. I was a little afraid to be in the same room with him, even if it was a public courtroom.

We were early and stopped for hot chocolate near the courthouse. When it came time to leave and walk up the steps to the court, I became nervous. At the door I put my bag down on the conveyor belt that carried it through an X-ray machine. I made the alarm on the metal detector scream and had to be checked by a guard with a handheld wand.

No one from the FBI or the prosecutor's office seemed to be around, so I walked up to the door and slowly opened it. As I looked in, the first person I saw was Frank. He was wearing a double-breasted suit and he was speaking with his attorneys. I didn't recognize him, but I knew it was him. There was something different about him, and I realized it was his glasses. He had worn contacts in Texas.

I stood in the doorway for just a few seconds, but it was

long enough for them to notice me. I couldn't see any familiar faces from our side, so I stepped back into the hall.

"He is in there," I told David. It was all real now, more real than it had ever been. In a moment the elevator door opened and the prosecution team walked out. I would be allowed to enter the courtroom with them, which I did. I sat with David behind their table. I looked at the defense and I saw Frank standing next to his lawyer. The lawyer was rubbing Frank's back, just like Frank had rubbed my back to guide me into the bathroom of his hotel room.

In front of me, Attorney Garrity-Rokous poured a glass of water. He winked at me as if things would be all right. I felt like they were going to be, and I felt satisfied that my ordeal was finally beginning to be over. I wanted closure more than anything else, and I hoped that this day would begin that stage.

There were two knocks on the door and everyone rose. When we sat down again, I looked over at the defense side and saw the only person who occupied a seat was a reporter. This may sound crazy, but I felt sorry for Frank. He had no one there to support him. Maybe he's suicidal, I thought. If I faced prison with no family or friends I would be suicidal. That thought made me feel something I had not expected to feel—guilt.

Frank's lawyer told the judge that he wished to change his plea to guilty. The judge followed up with questions. Once again Frank was very quiet. I felt upset when he answered no to the judge's question about whether he had a criminal history. He hadn't been charged with any other crimes, but he had certainly committed some. I wanted to get up and protest, Why can't we count these?

Mr. Garrity-Rokous then gave a brief summary of what kind of testimony would be given if in fact this would go to trial. He mentioned records of e-mails and telephone bills that would prove Frank had been in touch with me. He said that I would have to testify about his groping me in the hotel room, and that a lot of other people—including the Texas police officers—would testify about my condition after I came out of Frank's room.

Then Frank stood up, walked to the witness stand, and took an oath to tell the truth. The judge read the charges and asked, "How do you plead?"

"Guilty."

With that one word two years of investigation and repercussions were over. The judge announced that sentencing would be held in eighty days. The gavel came down with a sharp crack and we were all free to leave.

As Frank was led out by his attorney, I stood up behind the prosecutor's table. Mr. Garrity-Rokous put out his hand and as I took it he said, "Congratulations, Katie."

I imagined that I should feel vindicated, maybe even victorious, but I didn't. I was fully aware of the fact that Frank was going to prison, and I was happy to know that at least for a short time, he would not be able to seduce anyone else. But ultimately I couldn't help but think this was a real tragedy for everyone, including him.

"The press wants to speak with you," added Mr. Garrity-Rokous. Neither David nor I was interested in speaking, so the prosecutor agreed to tell the reporters we were not available. He turned to leave us, but suddenly stopped.

"The defendant's lawyer wants me to give you a message," he said. "Frank wanted to meet with you, to apologize."

I was shocked. How could he offer a sincere apology? He lived for the pursuit of young girls and boys. He could only be doing this for appearances. "Tell him to write me a letter," I said.

In the hallway I passed right by Frank and his lawyers. I looked at him and suddenly realized that one brief Sunday-morning chat on AOL had led to this. My life was a shambles, and he was going to jail. This says something about the power of the sickness that was inside of him. Getting to me— not me in particular, but just getting to a young girl—was so important to him that he had been willing to risk everything. Suddenly the anger that made me reject his request for a meeting melted, and it was replaced by regret. Maybe I should have let him talk to me. Maybe I owed him that much.

On the car ride home David was mostly silent and so was I. About halfway through the trip I clicked on the radio and started channel surfing. "Can't you stick with one station for at least thirty seconds?" snapped David.

"Don't yell at me," I said.

"Feeling guilty about screwing up a man's life?" he asked.

I was stunned into silence. I wanted to tell him he was wrong, that Frank had done it all to himself. But in that one sentence David had broken the fragile dam that was holding back all my inner doubts and fears. Yes, I did feel guilty, but it wasn't for him to say it, to make it real.

>>>

That night, my mother came home and I told her about the hearing. I knew she regretted not going, even though she didn't say so. The next day the newspapers reported the defense attorney's explanation for the guilty plea. Frank wanted "to remove any undue hardship from the victim or her family," he said.

More guilt flooded my heart in the days after the guilty plea. I knew I would have a chance to actually speak at the sentencing hearing and decided that writing my statement might help me clarify things in my mind. That statement would be the first time that I would talk to Frank in more than two years. And it would be far different from anything I had said to him before.

When I sat down and tried to let my innermost feelings speak, I didn't like what I heard. Instead of raging at Frank, I kept remembering that I had been part of the relationship. I had been charming in our conversations and willing to meet him in Texas. But while he was about to lose his freedom, perhaps for years, I wasn't being punished at all by the court. Something about this was wrong.

I knew that he was older than me—everyone said that was why he was being punished—but I still felt responsible. At the time I considered myself very mature for my age— maybe most thirteen-year-old girls think this way, but I truly believed it. The truth of the matter was that I should have known better.

I needed to confess. I needed to say that I was guilty, maybe even as guilty as the man who was going to go to jail for our relationship. I was a straight-A student, a nationally ranked swimmer, and an accomplished musician. I had friends and family who loved me. In getting involved with that man named Mark on the Internet, I had betrayed them.

Me, Again

>>>

I was one of the last people to arrive back at school after spring break. I tried hard to lose myself in work and activities. I began rowing crew and actually enjoyed the killer workouts on Turkey Pond. But while other members of the team seemed to be ravenous after burning so many calories, I just didn't have any appetite.

Crew and everything else helped me forget about Frank. But every time my mind was not fully engaged, I'd start thinking about the upcoming sentencing. Before I knew it an hour had passed. Homework took longer and longer to complete, and sleeping became more and more difficult.

Over the phone my mom picked up on a little of what I was going through. I'd say something about feeling guilty, and she'd argue with me. Almost every day I'd find a voice mail message from her reminding me that we had done the right thing in reporting and prosecuting Frank.

I knew we had done the right thing. He had to be charged and punished for what he did. But in the end, his confession and the time he would spend in jail would give him some sort of completion. He had done something bad.

He had been caught. He was paying for it. Then he would be freed.

What about me? I had done something bad. I had been caught, but there would be no public ceremony where I could admit my guilt. There would be no formal punishment for me, and because of this, there would be no public moment when my debt would be declared paid in full.

This is what I thought about all day long. At night I'd lie awake, remembering that night in Texas, thinking about how my mother had suffered, imagining Frank being led into a prison cell. I'd wake up feeling the bile rising in my throat and my stomach convulsing and I'd run to the bathroom.

I began not eating at most meals because I knew I was going to throw it up and it would hurt more. I'd telephone my mother and ask if she thought I might need some sort of help. After the experience with Psychologists One and Two my mom was pretty skeptical about me seeing another counselor.

"You can talk with friends, Katie. Maybe you can do that, and get yourself involved with things. Time will pass and you will feel better."

"I'm not sure that's going to work this time," I said. "What if it doesn't?"

"Keep the counseling as a last resort. Think of it as something that's there if you need it."

I knew, deep down, that my friends weren't enough. They couldn't possibly understand my feelings. Last resort or not, I needed help.

>>>

As I walked up the stairs to the health center I worried about who might see me going in, but inside I saw at least a dozen people waiting to be seen. I knew them all, and it made me feel better about going, because if they went, I could go, too.

I didn't have to say much other than I wanted to see a counselor and I preferred seeing a woman. The receptionist asked for my schedule, and I handed it to her.

"I really don't have anything available," she said as she handed it back to me.

I wasn't ready for this. I mean, just getting myself up the stairs and into the waiting room had been hard enough. We talked a little bit about how busy everyone was. Then she said she'd try to find an opening for me, perhaps in a few days. And there were some off-campus options. She was very friendly, and it wasn't her fault that everyone had full schedules. I thanked her and left.

Maybe my mother was right. For now, I would just try to get through each day. I would row, attend my classes, do my work. A normal routine would make me feel better.

>>>

"Pick something that interests you," my English teacher said. "Pick a topic that excites you, pick something that you want to explore further."

I was supposed to settle on something like "The Role of Women in the South" or "The History of Baseball." But I was fixated on pedophilia. I thought about it all the time. I wondered if people are born with it. Is it something that you might be able to control? Is it curable?

Of course, I didn't want to think about this. I mean, I was a sixteen-year-old from supposedly perfect New Canaan, Connecticut. I was supposed to be thinking about what dress I was going to wear to the next dance, or figuring out what the hyperbolic sine curve meant. But there I was, standing at my teacher's door, with child molesters on my mind.

I have always found doors without windows intimidating. I never want to feel as if I am interrupting something. So I just stood there for a while. I slipped off my signet ring, twisted it in my hand, and then looked at the scratches that blur the initials. I ran my hands through my hair a couple of times and noticed that it was falling out of my head. Enough stalling. I knocked on the door.

"Hi, Katie."

I walked in and took a seat in his office. Avoiding eye contact at all costs, I began to look at the pictures on his desk—the happy wife and kids.

"I have thought about it, and I think that I might want to write something along the lines of . . . well, I thought it would be interesting if I explored, and I really want to understand . . . well, I want to write about pedophilia."

"Interesting. You know, that is a very fascinating topic. Not many people really understand how it affects our society."

"I think it is something that really affects each and every one of us, even if we don't know it."

"I just heard about a man in Boston who was charged with bringing a minor to Mexico; you could begin your research there."

"I think I have something different in mind."

It wasn't a question of whether I should feel responsible or guilty. I wanted to know how *much* guilt I deserved to feel. Frank was not pure evil. For a while he had been my closest friend, maybe even the best adult friend I had ever had. No one had ever tried that hard to know me, to understand me. I thought he must be sick, mentally disturbed. And I must have had something to do with it, too. But how much was me? How much was Frank? How much was this disease called pedophilia?

Of course, it was my choice to call it a disease and always use the proper word—*pedophilia*—instead of child molesting, or abuse, or assault. The word gave me shelter through clinical explanations, but it also came closer to what I had experienced. "Philia"—love—was somehow part of everything that had happened. The friendship and the excitement were as real as the shame. I didn't know if it was wrong for me to see it this way, but there it was.

>>>

It didn't surprise me that out of the sixty thousand books in the school library not one explained pedophilia. St. Paul's School has lots of old bricks and white clapboard, two chapels, but no books on pedophilia. It also didn't have a lot of books about homosexuality or AIDS.

If the library had rewarded me with a book or two, I might have been able to keep the whole thing at a safe distance. But when I came up dry, I turned to a special source, my own FBI agent. He could bring me closer to my essay topic. I didn't think much about how close. I just dialed.

As the phone rang in my ear I looked down at my fingers and then bit my hangnails. If I kept my hands busy, I couldn't hang up.

"Hi, Ron, it's Katie Tarbox."

(I have to admit I didn't know what to call him. Mr. Barndollar, Special Agent, Ronald. I chose Ron because that is what my parents called him.)

"Hi Katie." His voice was friendly.

"I hope I'm not interrupting you because I can call back later."

"Anything for you, Katie, any time's a good time. What's up?"

"Well, I'm writing a research paper about pedophilia, and I'm having an awfully difficult time finding resources. I want to use my case in it, although I'm not going to reveal that I am the victim in the case. [Victim. There's another word I'm ambivalent about.] So I guess I am looking for any records that you can give me."

Ron said I could have most of the records. He also promised to send me some books on how detectives investigate pedophile cases. But I wanted more.

"Can I get the interviews and the polygraph records?"

I knew these wouldn't benefit my paper in any way. But I needed them.

"Not a problem. I will send it all to you."

Ron paused for moment. I didn't say anything.

"By the way, how are you doing? David and I talked and he mentioned that you were feeling guilty. You have absolutely no reason to feel any guilt at all. You should feel proud that you have pursued this to the end."

Ron spent a long time, and a lot of words, trying to convince me that Frank was a monster and I was truly his victim. He told me about Frank's history of seducing teenage girls—and at least one thirteen-year-old boy—into sexual relationships. Intellectually, I had always assumed there were others. But until this moment I hadn't really believed it.

It turns out that besides owning an investment company, Frank did telemarketing out of a small office in California. He hired underage kids, mostly girls, and paid them cash under the table. According to Agent Barndollar, every once in a while he would choose someone to be employee of the month, and she—it was always a she—would get dinner out with him. Then he would manipulate her into going to his house, where he would take advantage of her.

Even though the same kind of thing had happened to me, I had a hard time believing it. It was even harder to accept what Ron said about some of the parents of these girls. They didn't file charges because they liked him.

"They don't feel as if their kids have been abused," continued Ron. "They view him as a positive role model in their kid's life. He used to take out girls on a date. He would show up at the house in his BMW convertible, nicely dressed, and you know how he looks, Katie. Physically he is not a very overbearing person, not to mention he looks extremely young. He would meet the parents before taking their daughter out."

"And they approved of this?"

"Katie, this is not all happening in New Canaan, Connecticut, where everyone has graduate degrees and earns millions a year. These are blue-collar towns, so for some of these families having a daughter dating a young professional was a very positive thing in their opinion."

I tried to use my head, my intellect, to make some sense of it. "So it is kind of like in ancient Greece," I said. Pederasty was accepted then because it pulled the youth into the upper classes.

"Somewhat. So he would take this girl and they would hop in the car and he would conveniently forget his wallet. This required that they return to his house before going to dinner, which was the original plan. Frank would take the girl up to his bedroom where he said his wallet would be, put on a whole act of searching frantically for the wallet that was always in his back pocket from the start. When the moment was right, he would then pin the girl down. The worst part was he would just drive her home afterward, acting like nothing happened."

There was more. Frank had used alcohol to get some girls to have sex with him, and he had run his number on at least one boy. He had even taken a few girls for vacations at Disney World.

"He is truly a bad person," said Ron. "And you are not bad at all."

I disagreed.

>>>

I can't really remember walking to the St. Paul's music building later that April morning. It was only the repetition of having gone there so many times that directed me down the paths. I didn't think about it, and once again I tried to distance myself from what was happening. If this meant having to drain all emotion out of my body, then I did it. I didn't have time to think about this, or so my mother told me.

As I walked down the paths I felt cold, even though it was around eighty degrees outside. I was so completely lost that when I looked over at the pond for a second I thought it was iced over. It was only after a third glance that I reassured myself it was in fact just a pond. All around me, people were enjoying the first warm spring day. They sat by the pond talking and laughing.

Without my mother there telling me to forget about it all, I didn't know how I should feel. As independent as I try to be, I like it when people tell me what I should do, and then I feel that I am doing things right. I have been this way my whole life. The FBI agent had just told me that Frank was evil and that I shouldn't feel guilty. But if I wasn't supposed to feel guilty, then what was I supposed to feel?

I walked into the lesson room and tried to force Frank out of my mind.

"Katie, how's it going?"

"Great," I lied.

"Are we ready to play a little Chopin's 'Revolutionary Etude'?"

I took out my music, placed it on the piano, and then just sat there, staring, frozen. My piano teacher probably assumed I was trying to focus on the music. In truth, the longer I sat there the more my mind wandered away from the music, from this room, from St. Paul's.

"I hope I am going to hear this *today.*"

And so there was my cue to begin and somehow forget Frank. I placed my hands on the keys. The next thing I knew, I was banging my head on the piano and crying.

"I am so sorry, but I just can't do this."

My teacher suggested that I go back to the dorm and rest, maybe take a shower. He might have said something else, but I rushed out before I could hear anything more. I kept thinking back to Frank and how he'd asked me to play the piano the night we decided to meet.

I passed all the same happy people on the way to the dorm. They were soaking up sun. I was thinking about Frank. Why did he choose me? If it all boiled down to sex, or so I had been told, then why couldn't he have just hired prostitutes? I didn't understand why it was me.

After I reached my room, I decided that maybe I should take a shower. Perhaps it would help.

The next thing I realized was that I was under the flowing water and it was cold. I reached out to adjust the water. I looked down and noticed I was still fully dressed. My black chenille sweater was slowly disintegrating. I felt like my physical self was falling apart, too. The only thing that seemed solid, and real, was the overwhelming guilt I felt.

I didn't know exactly how long I had been there, how I

had gotten there, and, more important, why I was standing there in my khakis, sweater, and shirt.

For some reason, I didn't take off my clothes when I realized this. I just took a shower as if it were any other time. If I didn't admit what was happening, maybe I wouldn't have to acknowledge that I was falling apart.

I put my hands against my face, pulled back my hair and put some shampoo in my hand. I washed my hair and rinsed it. I stood there for a long time before I finally turned off the water, got undressed, and dried myself with a towel. From the bathroom I went to the dryer to put my clothes in it. As I closed the lid, I began to cry once again.

>>>

My hair was still wet when I walked to the health center. The receptionist looked at me as if I were some kind of Halloween ghoul.

"I've been vomiting a lot lately, and not sleeping, and I just sort of came to, standing in the shower with my clothes still on. I don't know what's happening to me. Do you think I could see someone?"

"Yes, of course, sit down and you'll be next," she said.

"Could I use the phone to call my mom?"

"Of course you can."

I started to cry again when I heard her voice. When I was able to speak I told her that I was the most horrible person on this planet and that I needed to go to jail more than anyone else.

"That's not true, Katie," she said. "You are one of the best people I know."

"I have done so many horrible things."

"None of it was your fault."

"I don't understand how I could have ruined my life this

way," I said. "I had so much potential, but I threw it all away."

My mother agreed with my decision to see a counselor and told me she loved me. I then went to the waiting room and sat down. *Jerry Springer* was on the waiting room TV and the topic was "Teens and Their Lovers." A twelve-year-old girl was involved with a thirty-five-year-old guy. Her mother fell for the guy, too, so they just made it a ménage à trois.

As I watched, I began to think the entire world was a sex-crazed mess. I know *Jerry Springer* is entertainment, but what are you supposed to think when grown-ups make a twelve-year-old the object of their desire and then go on TV to talk about it like it's normal? When my mother was a kid, she came home to reruns of *Father Knows Best*. I get transsexuals, hookers, and pedophiles. Sometimes this makes me laugh. This time, it made me feel dirty.

>>>

The counselor's name was Vivian, not doctor-something, but just Vivian. She was a small woman about forty years old, with long black hair and brown eyes that were very wide open, kind and trusting. She told me she knew a little of what was going on, but it would be best if I explained it. I couldn't look her in the face, so I stared at the floor as I spoke.

"Well, I met a man on the Internet. I mean, I didn't know he was a man at first, I thought he was just a guy. Anyway, we planned to meet in Texas during this swim meet. I went to his hotel room and he molested me."

"Okay."

"Now I'm involved in this trial. It's been going on for a long time and I guess I just kind of lost it under the pressure."

"Why now?"

"I think it's because I've got nobody to talk to. I mean,

nobody in my family has been really able to talk about it, and there's no one here."

"It's pretty understandable. I mean, these things do happen, but most people are pretty shocked and don't know what to say at all. It's very hard to talk about being molested."

"You're not shocked?"

"No, I'm not shocked. Have you tried talking to someone like me before?"

"Once. She was lame. She didn't offer me anything. She just wanted me to talk for an hour. She just sat there."

"I'm not going to just sit here."

"What are you going to do?"

"I'm going to help you understand that this is not your fault."

"Oh yeah, right."

>>>

The truth was, Vivian had already made me feel a little better. She was the first person who didn't seem disgusted by my story. She wasn't shocked, either, by the fact that I had come unglued emotionally. I walked away feeling better. It was all out, and now I really had someone to talk to. She even gave me her home number, in case of an emergency.

I walked back to my dorm and found Penn waiting in our room. I was desperate for a normal conversation— nothing about me and my problems—and I knew Penn could do that. I sat down and she complained to me about a trip her family was planning. They were going to go to a dude ranch in Wyoming and she really didn't want to go. I was happy to listen to somebody else's problems, and later we watched TV and laughed.

The next few days were difficult. I still didn't eat or sleep much. My parents offered to come up to see me, but I just didn't want to be a burden. My mom didn't settle for this answer. She left messages saying she couldn't just leave me at school in this condition. She had spoken to several doctors and they suggested I needed medication to help me cope. David said that if I allowed him to come up, he wouldn't bother me, just as long as he could make sure I would be okay. I said no to all of this, because I wanted to handle things on my own. It was almost as if I knew I had to suffer, and save myself, if I was going to feel redeemed for what I had done. My parents finally stopped pressing the issue when I promised to continue counseling and look into medication.

Talking with Vivian was very easy. She had spoken with my parents and sensed the power problem David has and how my mom could be an intimidating person. It was as if she already knew my family. I discussed my life during my swimming phase, which was basically no life. She then asked me whether I felt like I had control over my life. "Yes," I said, "very much so."

She didn't accept this. "Actually, you have been controlled all your life," she said. "It may be hard to realize, but you have." I may have felt independent and strong at times, but I had always been ruled by the schedules and demands of other adults around me. Frank had been the ultimate example of this, controlling me, manipulating me, without me even realizing it. He had controlled me by first winning and then violating my trust.

I wanted to argue with her. Frank may have been a manipulator, but I was stronger than Vivian thought, and I had to take responsibility. All of New Canaan seemed to agree with this, even my family. I told her what my sister had said: I wasn't some girl who was randomly raped in the park. I wasn't allowed to play the innocent party. I told her what

David had said: "Feeling guilty about screwing up a man's life?"

Time and time again I heard Vivian reply, "Katie, you are not guilty."

Hearing this so much made me consider believing it. And with Vivian I was finally able to admit that I had feelings for Frank. Even though I had friends who were sexually active, they didn't have romantic feelings for a person who was old enough to be their father. Vivian said I didn't need to explain, it was easy to understand.

I said it was sinful. She laughed. "It would have been hard not to have deep feelings for him," she said.

Vivian agreed that I should see a psychiatrist to prescribe medication to help me through the term. I was terribly afraid of this, but I knew that depression was not unusual. Almost everyone experiences it at some time.

My mother asked me repeatedly if I really needed to see a psychiatrist. I thought I did, but she said, "You know, it would really be better if you could figure things out yourself, Katie."

"I can't, Mom, I'm only sixteen," I said.

At the doctor's office I filled out forms explaining everything that I had done. When we finally met, she asked me my life's history, paying particular attention to sex.

"Are you sexually active?"

"No, I'm only sixteen."

"Well, you never know these days."

"I am a virgin."

She prescribed an antianxiety medication that would "take the edge off of things." That sounded good to me.

It was Good Friday, and when I got back to the dorm my parents picked me up so we could go to Boston for Easter. I missed my parents terribly, and I was thrilled about seeing them. It was also my mom's birthday, so my older sister was going to come up from college. Seeing my family together and happy for the first time in a long time was really good for me.

On Easter Sunday my mother hid a bunch of Godiva Easter eggs in the hotel room and we hunted for them. Back when we dyed our own eggs at Easter nobody wanted to find them because we all hated eating them. Hunting for Godiva eggs was a little different.

At the end of the day I didn't want to go back to school because I didn't want to leave my mom. My sister drove me back, and on the trip we made fun of my parents and she let me change the radio station as often as I liked. Abby dropped me off and kissed me good-bye. When I went up to my room, my new medication was waiting.

I was still afraid to take it, afraid to go to counseling, ashamed to think I had a "mental illness." Like my mother always does, I made a list of the pros and cons. Taking the pills meant I no longer had control over my own body, but at the same time I realized I had a problem. I swallowed the pill.

>>>

Together Vivian and I worked on how I felt and how I thought about myself and what had happened. She helped me understand why I had loved the man who called himself Mark, and why a part of me loved him still. I was also able to see that he wasn't real. Mark was like a character created by a gifted writer. He was a product of the Internet and Frank Kufrovich's malevolent imagination, and it was Mr. Kufrovich who was going to jail.

This made it much easier for me to handle the letter that he sent to me (and is now part of the court record) a few days prior to his sentencing.

Dear Katie,

I have wanted to write this letter for two years, but as the time nears for the day when I hope you can finally put the events of March 12, 1996, out of your mind forever, I thought it was appropriate to say in words what I've wanted to say in-person for so long: I'm so very sorry . . . I was wrong . . . you share no blame . . . and I pray that you and your mother and entire family are at peace.

Over the last two years, I've been giving intensive care to my very ill 83-year-old mother. I mention this, because I've had a long and sobering opportunity to see how events of one person's life can have a very profound and material impact on another's. What I mean to say is that I now realize how my careless and totally thoughtless actions towards you caused you untold anguish.

I know that telling you that I've cried almost daily for this anguish you've suffered sounds self serving, but nevertheless it's true . . . I have. If I could only change the past, I hope you know that I would. You were the innocent party here. For that I am truly sorry beyond the mere words I am writing today.

I was the adult, not you. I should have acted like an adult. You were not at fault here. I know that you already know this, but I wanted to say this myself to remove any shred of doubt, and I hope you will remember it always.

At my hearing about two weeks ago [March 13, 1998], in the courtroom and after the hearing, I asked my attorney to ask your representatives if they would convey my deepest apologies, and additionally asked for a moment to personally (with your supporters present with you) say these things to you. I was told after a conference discussion that you were not emotionally prepared to hear my apology at that time.

I felt that it might possibly help the healing process for you to hear my in-person apology, and that it might bring some closure and (perhaps) some degree of peace to you.

Katie, I'd still like the opportunity to meet for a moment (with your parents, prosecution, or counselor present, of course) to let you see just how sorry I am.

I will not try to make any statement to you other than an apology, so as not to make you feel ill at ease, and will depart immediately. You can rely on this promise, and if you have any doubts, can confirm with the Probation Department that I have kept all my promises thus far, if you wish.

I can see you almost any day that you feel this would be helpful, or perhaps a convenient day would be the day before the next court hearing in June, or perhaps alternatively one hour before the actual hearing itself. What might be best for you?

I hope that you might consider this opportunity a less stressful time for hearing my apology, separately from the more public courtroom events, although I will apologize publicly there also. I can understand if your answer is "no," and if this is the case, please consider this my last and final contact with you and your family. I hope you might say yes, and that nevertheless you can put my terrible mistake in proper perspective over the days and months to come.

Please don't be surprised when I say that I pray you will have only success and happiness for the rest of your life. These are my feelings . . . No one assisted me in writing this letter.

I'm sincerely hoping you can feel the sincerity of my words. I truly mean them. You've suffered *enough, and I hope God rewards your intelligence, talents, and obvious inner strength with nothing but the joys you truly deserve, and have every right to expect, throughout your successful life.*

God bless you, Katie.

This letter wasn't written to me, it was written directly to the judge. He was only writing that letter to try to look like a decent person. The only thing that he wanted me to feel toward him was pity. I think he wanted me to feel bad that he was going to jail and that I was taking him away from his sick mother.

The only thing that upset me was his desire to apologize to me in person. There was no way I could say yes to that, but I worried that this made me a bad person. He wasn't asking for forgiveness, just a chance to apologize, and because I didn't give that to him, I felt bad. He didn't deserve that chance, but it was very difficult for me to say no.

>>>

Frank Kufrovich did eventually see me one last time. It was at his sentencing hearing in a courtroom that was much more crowded than it had been for his guilty plea. He had brought several character witnesses, including his Catholic high school principal from Pennsylvania. They all got up and said what a good man he was. Imagine that, a school principal pleading on behalf of a pedophile. Then Frank spoke for himself. He begged for pity. I refused to look at him.

When it was my turn, I rose with a strange mixture of anxiety and confidence. I started speaking fast, reading from a statement I had put on paper. The judge interrupted, asking me to slow down. I did, and I told them about how Frank Kufrovich had stolen two years of my life, two years of my childhood, that I could never get back. I told them about the pain I had suffered, the guilt and shame. And I told them that I was lucky to have a family and friends and school that helped me through it all.

"He is not worthy of being a member of our society," I said. "It is not a God-given right. A citizen has expectations and responsibilities to meet. When these basic requirements are not met I think it is vital for the institutions of this country to protect our society. . . . I am looking up to you," I told the judge, "because you alone have the authority to determine how this man is going to spend the next few years of his life."

When the judge ruled that Frank Kufrovich would be incarcerated for eighteen months, it meant absolutely nothing to me. I don't think I cared because I didn't know what a fair sentencing was for a pedophile. I also didn't want to think that this was the price for my suffering.

Outside in the hallway I saw Frank surrounded by his supporters. I stopped and stared until Agent Barndollar touched my shoulder and said, "You did good."

Epilogue

>>>

As Agent Barndollar said, I did good in that courtroom. But the pain I continued to feel inside told me I hadn't done enough. I still felt empty and confused, like part of me was still his victim. I needed to do something public, something that would destroy all the secrecy and maybe, in the process, lift my shame. The shame would only go away when the truth was told and accepted by everyone who was important to me. This had happened with the people at the courthouse and inside my family. All that was left was my community at St. Paul's.

Four times each week, everyone at St. Paul's takes an assigned seat in the chapel for a ritual that has been going on for more than one hundred years. It always includes a reading from Scripture, a presentation of some sort—a speaker, skit, or performance—followed by a hymn and a prayer. Nobel Prize winners and presidents have come to speak at the chapel. When the rector suggested that I might like to speak in chapel, I knew it was the right thing to do.

So on a September afternoon, after the Scripture was read, I stepped up to the pulpit to face about six hundred of my peers and my teachers. I began by reading them a news-paper article that summarized the case of the *United States of America v. Frank Kufrovich*. The article said that "the victim, who now attends an exclusive boarding school, told Senior U.S. District Judge Ellen Bree Burns that 'Kufrovich robbed me of two years of my life.' "

When I finished reading the article, I paused for a moment, took a breath, and then continued:

"Two years ago I didn't really know what a pedophile was. I am still not sure how some of the events took place. I couldn't have known I was beginning a two-year struggle.

"The pedophile who went after me threatened to hurt me and my family if I disclosed any of the events that hap-pened to me. Following the incident I was immediately con-fronted with the hardest decision of my life, to press charges or keep this information hidden to myself and live my life pretending as if nothing had ever happened.

"I went almost a week without notifying my parents or any authorities. I literally felt as if I were guilty of everything that he was guilty of. I know if it weren't for my conscience, I probably would have let this go.

"You may think, as I do now, How could anyone let something like this go? I can tell you that ninety percent of these cases are not recognized because victims—who feel afraid, ashamed, guilty, and even responsible—will not speak. . . .

" . . . After I formally pressed charges I was called to give reports at an FBI office. I had a polygraph test. I testified at a grand jury. The hardest part for me was beyond the court-room doors and interview rooms. The FBI strictly admonished me to only speak of this matter if absolutely necessary. Even to this day, I am not allowed to reveal all of the details.

"But I can tell you that this case has affected me every day of my life and affects many decisions that I have to make today. I lost many of my closest friends at home. Keeping this hidden affected my health, and worst of all, my sense of myself. At times I even lost faith in myself as a person.

"Through all of this, I learned many valuable lessons. I have learned how to be tenacious through the judicial system. I have learned that life is not fair. I have learned to believe in myself. I have learned that how a person handles setbacks really speaks a lot about their character. I have learned that nothing good in life should be taken for granted. . . .

". . . I am now trying to take the most horrible situation in my life and turn it into the most positive aspect of my life. And I believe that this represents a great accomplishment. As JFK once said, 'A mistake doesn't become a mistake unless it goes uncorrected.' Life is not about setbacks, but how you overcome them."

I stood at the podium for a few moments as I began to see people put their hands together and clap. I then saw a few people from various parts of the chapel stand up. I began to cry when I saw my friends stand up and cheer. Finally, I was no longer a victim.

>>>

A year after I spoke at chapel, I am now preparing to go to college. At boarding school I still use the Internet, for communication and research. It is a wonderful way to keep in touch with people. In fact, much of this book was transmitted, in one form or another, over the Internet. At home, my parents continue to let me use AOL—I guess they figure I've learned my lesson—but my sister Carrie, now thirteen years old herself, isn't allowed anywhere near the Net.

Of course, the Internet was only one factor in what happened to me. I was also affected by my own insecurities, by my isolation from my family, and by the sexual pressures that all young girls experience. A little older, and a lot wiser, I am better able to choose my own path. I am stronger.

I can't say that thirteen-year-old girls in general are any stronger than they were four years ago. I can see on television, and hear in the conversations that adults have, that a lot of people are worried about adolescent girls. Unfortunately, I don't see or hear anything being done to help them. Parents still prefer to deny that thirteen-year-olds live in a sex-saturated world. New Canaan is still a place where physical beauty is valued over everything else.

I am shocked by how much Carrie struggles and yet denies that anything difficult is going on. I know she is confused about boys and dating and sex, and yet she doesn't even admit any of this. It is almost like she thinks that talking about it is wrong. She doesn't understand, and nobody seems to be able to help her understand, that *not* talking about it is really dangerous.

I cannot offer a prescription for a society that seems to value girls as objects and sets them up for the kind of predator who invaded my life. I can only tell you what might help your friends, your sister, your niece, your neighbor, or your daughter.

Understand the world she lives in. It is more adult than you can ever imagine, and the pressures she faces would be difficult for any grown woman to handle.

Let her be heard. Every girl says she is doing fine. But if you just spend the time, you might hear the rest of the story. And if she just won't talk to you, give her a chance to connect to another adult. In the time after Frank, I have gotten help from teachers and counselors who were much easier to face than my own parents.

Let her know she's not alone. The shame I felt when I

was thirteen came about because I thought I was alone in how I felt.

Help her see her own value. Too many girls seem willing to believe that their worth is determined by other people. The Internet has created a new avenue for the predators who would exploit this insecurity. Girls who have goals, real connections to family and friends, and a sense that a world of opportunity awaits them seem to be inoculated against this danger. I feel that way now. I wish I had felt that way back then. Before.

>>>

Suggestions for protecting your child while on-line:

- Never allow children unsupervised access to the Internet. Keep the computer in a common area of your home, not a child's bedroom. Periodically and without warning, observe what they are doing.

- Learn about the blocking mechanisms provided by your Internet provider and by software manufacturers. Use them to keep children out of adult chat rooms or sexually permissive sites.

- Tell your children never to give out information such as phone numbers, addresses, last names, names of schools, or activities they participate in.

- Remind children that whatever they are told by others on-line may not be true. A twelve-year-old girl may actually be a fifty-year-old man.

- Never allow a child to upload his or her picture to someone.

- Instruct your child never to arrange a face-to-face meeting with someone they have met on the Internet.

- Monitor the time your child spends on the Internet and the duration of the session.

- Monitor your phone bills.

- Advise your child never to respond to messages that are suggestive, obscene, or harassing. Encourage the child to report to you any messages that make him or her feel uncomfortable, then forward a copy of the message to your Internet provider's consumer department.

- Spend time at the computer with your children and build their self-esteem. Tell them to teach you how to use the computer and ask them to show you where they go and who they talk to. If there are suspicions, check the e-mail they have received.

(Reprinted with permission from Michael P. Mayko, *Connecticut Post*. Source: the FBI and the National Center for Missing and Exploited Children.)

>>>

Before going, I'd like to recommend a list of Internet sites that can be beneficial in helping to make the Internet a safe place.

1. www.bess.net
2. www.gulliver.nb.ca
3. www.librarysafe.com
4. www.ourworld.compuserve.com
5. www.xstoop.com
6. www.machinasaplens.qc.ca
7. www.intergo.com/tour/kguard
8. www.cyberpatrol.com
9. www.solidoak.com/cysitter.html

ACKNOWLEDGEMENTS

ACKNOWLEDGMENTS

>>>

I feel very blessed to have so many influential people in my life. It is their inspiration that has made *Katie.com* come to life.

I would first like to thank my family—Abby, Carrie, Mom, and Dave—whose love has been the greatest gift. Their support has guided me through a very stressful time in my life, and their faith in me has allowed me to finish this book. Thank you for understanding when the laptops crashed, flying down to Washington, D.C., to let me write, and giving me the freedom and space to complete this. Many thanks also to my grandmother for her love, support, and interest. A special tribute goes to my grandfather, who passed last June, but will always be remembered for performing duties well over and above anyone's expectations and, most important, for sharing with me his great sense of humor, which is so valuable in my life.

My appreciation goes to my many friends who had to put up with me while I was writing. My good friend Tara Tunney deserves some type of reward for having endured my endless jabbering. Tara, thanks for all the great talks and a summer to remember in Washington, D.C. Penn Whaling receives special recognition for actually living in a room with me while I spent endless hours on the phone and late nights at my computer. Thank you, Penn, for your sense of humor, which has kept me laughing every day. Courtney Folgeman, thank you for your understanding nature and sharing your Doritos with me when I needed comfort at stressful times. I would like to thank Kerry Brandon, Mimi Mayer, Kristen George, Lina Schuerch, Lisa Farewell, and Katie Calhoun for graciously listening to me talk about this. I would also like to thank my fellow pages in Washington, D.C.

I owe much gratitude to many fine teachers who helped me along the way: Mrs. Hackett, Dr. Gerardo-Gettens, Mrs. Anna Mase, Mrs. Poltrack, Ms. Gesualdi, Mrs. Lisa Smith, Dr. Marshall, Ms. Barker (especially her hot fudge sauce), and Bishop Anderson. I would most especially like to thank Mr. Carlisle, who showed me what good writing really looks like and helped me to develop my writing voice.

I would also like to thank my attorney, Alan Neigher, who is one of the main reasons Katie.com is here. Thank you for your faith in my story and writing and your support throughout. Thank you to my agent, BJ Robbins, whose dedication has helped make Katie.com a success. Without your help, I would be completely lost in the publishing world.

Thank you to my editor, Laurie Chittenden, whose energy and enthusiasm have made this an exciting project. I am so lucky to have had the opportunity to work with someone who has so much insight and intelligence. Last, but certainly not least, my deep gratitude goes to Michael D'Antonio for making sure that I wrote every single day, but most especially for leading me to places that I didn't think I could reach as a writer at seventeen.